copy.

C000064729

righter.

copy.

righter.

Ian Atkinson

London   Madrid
New York   Mexico City
Barcelona Monterrey

Published by
LID Publishing Ltd.
6-8 Underwood Street
London N1 7JQ (United Kingdom)
Ph. +44 (0)20 7831 8883
info@lidpublishing.com
LIDPUBLISHING.COM

A member of BPR

businesspublishersroundtable.com

Printed in Great Britain by TJ International Ltd.

ISBN: 978-1-907794-14-8
Collection editor: Jeanne Bracken
Cover illustration: © Glen Marsden 2011
Typesetting: SyS Alberquilla S.L.

First edition: July 2011

Contents

Introduction

You learn to write when you're what, four or five?

It's that easy.

Which means by the time you start work, you're something of an expert.

And of course you want people to realise just how clever and brilliant you are.

So you make sure your writing is full of complex ideas. You use a few long words (including the latest terminology) and you sprinkle in a little of your creative genius.

Et voila! You're a pretty gifted wordsmith.

At least, that's what many people seem to think about themselves.

Which is a little odd really.

Because they know that the ability to turn on a tap doesn't make them a plumber.

And that being able to change a fuse doesn't make them an electrician.

Yet they don't realise that the ability to bash out a few sentences while a red wiggly line underlines their spelling mistakes doesn't make them an expert copywriter.

We'll look at what does.

We'll look at how to grab your reader's attention and keep them enthralled. Style. Structure. Substance. The role of emotion. The benefits of wit. Writing in different media. Writing for different brands. Easy examples, handy hints and tasty tricks to quickly improve your copywriting.

But most of all, we'll explore how to change someone's behaviour.

How to persuade someone to do what you want them to do – just using the power of the written word.

And you can, you know. The world's best copywriters do it all the time.

This book will show you how.

Ready? Then let's get cracking.

1 The Fantastic Four
How to write good copy

1.1 How to write purposefully
specific objective, universal objective, clarity & focus

1.2 How to write practically
punctuation, grammar, typography & layout

1.3 How to write pleasingly
Aristotle, audience, tone & interest

1.4 How to write persuasively
WIIFM, Maslow, motivation & emotional vs rational

In the next section, *The Famous Five,* we'll look at the skills you need to craft great copy from scratch – exploring ideas such as insight, brand, concept, storytelling and personality.

But in this section, *The Fantastic Four,* we're going to start off slow. We'll explore the basics, so you can write (or critique) good copy that's grounded in four important principles.

Copywriting that has purpose, is practical, pleasing and persuasive.

How to write purposefully

specific
objective,
universal
objective,
clarity
& focus

i. The specific objective

Watch a puppy in a new house. They bound around, tail wagging, tongue lolling, ears flapping up and down as they dart everywhere. Enthusiastically sniffing everything.

Then – woah! They're entranced by your slippers. Your slippers are the most exciting, most important thing in the – wait, what's this? An old newspaper! Yes, that's the most amazing thing I've ever seen! I could play with this forever, I – ooh, a tennis ball!

Copy can be like that. All over the place. Lacking direction and purpose.

But good copy is written to meet a specific, stated objective. Which sounds obvious – but there's plenty of work that seems written for no reason other than to fill some white space. Or because 'We need something about our new product launch to go out.'

You need to know what the aim is. A clear, identified and agreed objective which you stick to – like a pneumatic, permatanned blonde to a footballer in a nightclub.

Before you start writing (or reviewing) copy, make sure you know what this objective is. Have it written somewhere clearly, something like 'The aim is to persuade our audience to book a free test drive of our new car, the Ferrari 840.'

How you achieve that objective through the power of your writing is what the rest of this book is about. But a simple, singular, specific objective is an important start.

If you don't know what the objective is, one thing's for sure: you haven't much hope of achieving it.

So if you're not clear, speak to whoever you're writing for; it saves a lot of time in the long run. Believe me – I've been in meetings where the client has said, "Yeah, it's great and everything… but it's not really what I was expecting" and over the course of the next 20 minutes we've discovered that what they wanted isn't what we thought they wanted.

Because it had never been that clear in the first place.

In Part 2 of this book we'll take this on a step – from a blunt *objective* to a razor-sharp *proposition*. But for now, a single-minded objective is a vital start. Make it the very first thing you write and make sure everyone's in agreement before you start.

There's an acronym people use for personal performance objectives – SMART. 'Specific, Measurable, Achievable, Realistic and Time-bound'. They're useful here too: is your objective SMART?

Handy hint

ii. The universal objective

As well as the specific objective, there's always a second, universal objective for every piece of copy you write. It's this: to communicate with *style* and *substance*.

In fact, to write with a style that *serves* the substance.

Much copy is written with one (and sometimes both) of these missing.

Copy that only has substance (content) is often dull. And, as most people are exposed to over 4,000 messages a day, no-one's going to read what's dull.

As famous ad man David Ogilvy once said, "You cannot bore someone into buying your product."

And we've all read copy that's just substance. Where the writer is so in love with their subject, they don't bother trying to make it interesting and tasty. They just ladle it out in thick, unappetising chunks and they never bother to add seasoning.

On the other hand, you'll see plenty of copy that's written with very little substance. Some of the books I've read on copywriting, for example, were disgracefully thin on content – just vague, wishy-washy drivel that didn't really tell you anything.

Good copywriters find out what's most interesting about their subject – and their copy is dense with great substance. If you haven't got anything interesting to say, go find something. Compose your copy using the best quality ingredients.

Meanwhile, you also see plenty of writing that's just about style. It's particularly common in the work of wannabe writers: people who think they have a gift for writing and want to impress you with their wordplay.

That's a very unhelpful starting point – to write with the aim of impressing your audience with your writing ability, when you should be trying to impress your audience with your content; the substance of your copy.

So: style and substance. Get the balance right and you'll communicate elegantly and effectively.

To go back to the food analogy, think of your copy as a stew. Too big a portion (substance) and you'll give your audience indigestion. Too little, and you'll leave them hungry and unsatisfied. No seasoning (style) and the meal is bland. Too much and it's inedible.

iii. Clarity & focus

We have our objectives.

That's *what* we're going to write; now *how* are we going to write?

Put simply: simply.

If the first tenet of writing with purpose is to have a specific objective and the second is to write with style and substance, this is the third. *To communicate as clearly and simply as you possibly can.*

It seems obvious, yet many 'amateur' writers think their writing should use long words and complex sentence construction. That every thought should be expressed in a way that only a clever audience could understand.

They're wrong.

There you go. The effectiveness of a two word, two syllable paragraph: 'They're wrong'.

The truth is, the more simply and clearly you speak, the better you will be heard.

In fact, one of a copywriter's most important jobs is often to 'Make the complex simple'. Spend time finding the pithiest, simplest way to express something.

Because *that's* clever. To write about a subject in a way that makes people say 'Oh, I'd never thought of it like that before', or 'I've never really understood it until now'.

Look at the instruction manual for any Apple product. Before Apple became so successful, other technology companies used to have vast, verbose instruction manuals in horrendous detail and off-putting language.

Apple made it simple. Crisp. Brief. They give you the quickest possible route to getting started and enjoying the product you've just bought from them. (Which they then make as simple as possible to use.)

Be like Apple. Find and express the simple truth behind a complicated idea. That's an achievement to be proud of. And cut out the flab so only the meat is left.

As Einstein said, "You do not really understand something unless you can explain it to your grandmother." Or, to quote advertising luminary Dave Trott, "Complicated isn't clever. It just looks clever to stupid people."

But a note of caution: what you're aiming for is copy that's simple, not simplistic.

Simplistic means you are 'over-simplifying' something, missing out key truths about it.

Simple copy means finding a way to distil the complexities of a subject into something anyone can understand, using everyday language.

Avoid jargon, acronyms, obfuscation, ambiguity and verbosity. Embrace clarity.

Aim for writing that is *dense but light*. Dense, because it has a lot of meaning and substance in every sentence. But light, because it's still easy to read, not turgid and taxing to wade through.

It's not easy to achieve. But it's a cornerstone of good copywriting.

Look at your first sentence or paragraph. What would you lose if you removed it?

Often, the answer is 'not much' and you'd be quicker into the meat of the story. Many people often 'warm up' to their theme as they start writing, but then don't go back and delete their warm-up exercises. So have a look: maybe your third line is the real, powerful opening you need, and you can just cut the two before it.

At the same time, write with focus. Which basically means staying true to the specific objective, not wandering off course. There are two common reasons for losing focus:

a) Multiple client objectives

Where the client wants you to mention four different products in one press ad. Or promote all eight benefits of their new service in a social media campaign.

This is a 'Can't see the wood for the trees' occasion. If you write about *everything*, chances are people won't take in *anything*. It's much more effective to focus on one subject than try and juggle several.

b) Having several interesting things to say

I was guilty of this when I first started writing a blog. Sometimes there'd be a week when more than one interesting thing happened to me (I know, I live quite the dilettante life).

So I'd find a way to get both stories into the same blog. After all, they were both individually interesting. Together they'd make the article twice as interesting, wouldn't they?

No. They just make it twice as busy and half as focused.

Again, don't fall in love with your own copy. Prune out anything that isn't helping the style and substance tell the story as powerfully as possible.

If it makes it easier, cut out the extraneous copy and save it in a document of 'leftovers' that you can tell yourself you'll re-use some time.

Though you probably won't.

Punctuation,
grammar,
typography
& layout

i. Punctuation & grammar

English is an evolving language.

We might not always like the way it evolves (I hate the way people say 'real' instead of 'really', for example).

But the alternative is to not evolve. Like French.

French is carefully regulated (by things like the *Toubon Law* and organisations like *L'Académie française*) and has a famously small vocabulary (excluding scientific and technical words, perhaps just 50,000 to our 250,000).

Which must make being a French copywriter rather tedious.

The trouble is, if you don't evolve you get left behind and end up with *nil points*.

So we have to get used to the constant mutation of the English language; new words like *screenager* (a teenager who lives online) and *staycation* (holidaying at home) appear, old ones like *egrote* (to feign an illness) die.

Punctuation and grammar change too, making it difficult to be definitive about what's right and wrong. But what we can agree on is the *purpose* of these things.

And it's still to communicate. As effortlessly as possible. Which means three things.

One, we should know the current, official guidelines for punctuation, grammar and spelling.

Secondly, we should bear in mind our audience.

If your audience is older and educated, they may not like split infinitives or sentences that begin with a proposition. In which case, don't do it – because good copy should get your audience on your side, not alienate them. However, most audiences won't mind (or even know about) such things.

Thirdly, good copywriting is often colloquial and conversational in tone. And people don't speak in perfectly arranged sentences – they play fast and loose with the rules of usage, frequently using sentences that don't contain a verb for example.

Fine. Your writing can too (like the preceding one word, verb-free sentence, for instance). It makes your copy more approachable, more engaging and easier to absorb.

In other words, spelling and punctuation you should *always* do correctly. Grammar you should *usually* do correctly. Usage… well, that's a more moveable feast.

Let's cover a few of the common mistakes in spelling, punctuation and grammar, including some that a spell-checker wouldn't pick up:

Could of

This is as a result of people writing what they hear. People say "could have" in a way that sounds like "could of". So you see "could of / would of / should of", when the correct phrase is "could have / would have / should have".

"Literal" for "metaphorical"

People say, "It literally blew my mind," when they mean the exact opposite – it *metaphorically* blew their mind. If it had literally blown their minds, they wouldn't be capable of talking about it.

"Their" for "there" or "they're"

"Their" means something that belongs to someone (like "their socks"), "there" is a place (like "you left your socks over there") and "they're" is just short for "they are" (like "those socks of yours, they're disgusting").

"It's" and "its"

The correct usage is very simple to remember, yet it's used incorrectly more and more. On BBC television news captions, for example. On film subtitles. In professional copywriter's drafts.

Here's the answer: "It's" is only ever used when it's short for "it is" or "it has". Otherwise use "its".

No need to think about possession or anything complicated like that. Just read the sentence, substituting the occurrence of "its" with "it is" (or "it has"). If it makes sense with "it is" / "it has", then you use "it's". If it doesn't make sense, use "its". And that's all there is to it.

"Your" and "you're"

Again, very simple. "You're" is short for "you are", so just see if the sentence makes sense with "you are", in which case use "you're". If not, use "your".

"Maybe" and "everyday"

"Maybe" and "may be" are not interchangeable. Substitute "maybe" for "perhaps" – if it makes sense, then ok. If not, then you mean "may be". For instance, "It may be right to change this, what do you think?" "Maybe."

Similarly, "everyday" means something is ordinary and commonplace. So if you take a vitamin tablet each morning, you're taking one "every day", not "everyday".

"Desert" for "dessert"

I saw this on a menu in a Lake District restaurant recently. I wanted to order one, but I was worried it might be a bit dry.

"Loose" for "lose"

You don't "loose" a game of golf, you "lose" it. Unless you win, of course.

CD's

You don't need the apostrophe. Or after TVs or 1000s or the 1990s any time you're just talking about the plural of something that has capital letters or numbers. However, using an apostrophe here isn't the end of the world and it's often done because sometimes it can make things clearer – for example, when the last letter is a vowel.

Parentheses

Or brackets, if you want to be common. If the open bracket starts during the sentence, then the full stop will finish outside the close bracket (like this). (However, if the open bracket starts before the first word, the full stop is inside the closing bracket, like this.)

Less or fewer

Less means "not as much". Fewer means "not as many". So because we're talking about "not as many people" rather than "not as much people", the correct usage is "fewer people", not "less people".

We say "less than two weeks" because "two weeks" is how much time we're talking about, not "how many time".

Use of 'a' or 'an' before 'h' words

Some would-be sticklers insist that words beginning with an "h'" should be preceded by "an" not "a", as in "an hotel" or "an historic occasion".

But actually, if the "h" is pronounced, use "a". Use "an" where the "h" isn't pronounced. So it's "an hour", but "a hotel".

Hopefully

Like most people nowadays, I use hopefully 'incorrectly'. I do know the correct usage though: to do something hopefully means to do it positively. Hopefully does not mean 'fingers crossed'.

However, this is where grammar becomes rather muddy: hopefully has been used in a "Hopefully we'll get to the station in time" kind of way for a hundred years, but some people still object to it. So if you're cultivating a pedantic personality, only use hopefully in a "We will pitch for the business hopefully and energetically" kind of way.

Momentarily

The UK usage means *for* a moment, as in "We all paused momentarily before agreeing". The US usage means *in* a moment, as in "I'll be there momentarily" – I'll be there soon, not I'll be there for a very short period of time.

Split infinitive

Let me finish with one more favourite of the pedant: the split infinitive. The most famous example was always from Star Trek, where the opening credits voiceover announced that their mission was "To boldly go where no man has gone before". You shouldn't split 'to go', it should be "To go boldly where no man (or, as it became, *no-one*) has gone before."

But the truth is, split infinitives are one of those rules that seem to have no purpose other than to keep sticklers occupied and I wouldn't worry about it too much if I were you.

That's enough on the basics of punctuation and grammar. The point with this stuff is to know what's important and what's not, how to avoid silly errors and how to be mindful of what will rub your audience up the wrong way.

There are infinite resources on the web; it never takes more than a few moments to find the answer to any spelling, punctuation or grammar query you have. Get a good grip of things like apostrophes (such as using with plurals, like "two weeks' notice") and you'll be fine.

For books on punctuation and grammar, some that I've read and found useful are John Humphreys' *Lost For Words*, R L Trask's *The Penguin Guide to Punctuation* and Lynne Truss's *Eats, Shoots and Leaves*.

Incidentally, if you google Lynne Truss you'll find a number of people who claim there are a fair few punctuation and grammar mistakes in her book.

For example, the subhead to the book is 'The Zero Tolerance Approach to Punctuation'.

Even I know that neither 'zero' nor 'tolerance' can work independently as adverbs to 'approach', so they should be hyphenated: zero-tolerance. Truss, a self-confessed stickler, gets her punctuation wrong… on the front cover of her book about punctuation.

Which just goes to show what an unrewarding, tough old game it can be.

ii. Typography

You may not have as much influence over typography as you'd like.

Most clients have clear visual identities and those identities usually specify which fonts you can use and how you can use them. However, it's still worth knowing the basics:

Legibility

Copywriters want their carefully crafted words to be as legible as possible. And so should their clients.

In print – especially long copy – that means serif typefaces (which is why magazines and newspapers use them).

The reason is, our eyes don't take in individual letters, they recognise word shapes. Serifs (by which I mean the little sticks on the ends of the letters, such as those on these words) make those shapes quicker to recognise.

Online, where copy tends to be shorter anyway, sans-serif fonts are often more legible (because screens are made up of pixels that sometimes don't cope with the detail of serifs very well, creating unclear shapes).

Having said that, sans-serif fonts seem to have taken over *everywhere* in the last decade – perhaps because Arial was the default font on so much software – so you'll see it in lots of printed long copy.

Which means if you want to stand out – and be more readable – choose a serif font.

Apart from serif or sans-serif, the other two key considerations for legibility are colour and size.

For colour, the starting point is: do you have black text on a white background or white text reversed out of a dark-coloured background?

Black text on white is much more legible in print than reversed out text. Reversed out is fine for headlines and short copy, but harder to read for long copy. And be very wary of art directors who want to put your lovely copy over a picture – it will be very hard to read, so most people won't bother.

A current trend is light grey text on a white background (especially online) – again, avoid. Unless what you've written isn't worth reading.

The font size is also important. 11 or 12 point is typically used for body copy. Again, art directors will often want to reduce it down to 10 point, to create more air: resist this urge (unless you're writing a book, in which case 10 point is common).

But similarly, if they tell you they have to reduce it to 10 point to fit all your copy in, then the answer is probably to reduce the amount of copy, not the font size. Better that people read all of your shorter copy than none of your longer copy – which will happen if it looks off-puttingly small and tightly packed.

For terms and conditions and caveats you can go down to 8 point, but anything smaller is likely to be illegible.

Also look at the leading (pronounced ledding). That's the size of the font that's used to determine the distance between each line of copy. For instance, '11 on 10' means the font is 11 point, but set in a line grid of 10 point, so it'll be very close together. '11 on 12' means it's still an 11 point font, but set to a 12 point grid – there'll be a wider gap between each line and it'll be easier to read.

Of course, *actual* size varies according to font. 11 point Palatino looks a lot smaller than 11 point Cooper Black, for example.

And bigger is not always better. Too big a font or too much leading can make your copy look clunky and disjointed and harder to take in – like sitting in the front row at the cinema. Making a 12 word heading so big it goes onto five lines is going to be more difficult to read than having it smaller over three lines.

Look for a size that is pleasing to the eye and easy on the eye.

Proportion

Two simple points about the proportion of your copy.

Firstly, try writing your copy in the proportionate size it's going to appear. It gives you a better idea whether or not your copy suits what it's been written for.

If you're writing a billboard, try having the headline and any other copy in the respective proportions to each other that they will be in the finished work.

It's often very revealing to see how your eight word headline looks when it's really big.

Secondly, look at how using copy proportionately in this way affects the way lines break. Particularly for headlines, for example. There's no point in writing a headline that makes it impossible to balance the words well. For instance:

Is this headline ok?

only really works if you can get it all on one line. There's nowhere neat to break it – you'd have to have:

Is this
headline ok?

or

Is this headline
ok?

which is even worse.

So, if 21 characters in the headline still means the font is big enough, then:

Is this headline ok?

is fine. But if you and the art director decide that 12 characters across a headline is the most you'd really want then you may want to re-write it, to:

How's this
headline?

perhaps. Which balances much better – the first line is 10 characters long, the second 9.

I try and get my headlines to break at a point that not only balances them well physically, but which doesn't break the line in the middle of a phrase – for instance:

Get a free
gift today

balances very well in terms of length, but it splits the phrase 'free gift', which makes it more awkward to read. Instead:

Claim your
free gift.

breaks more logically.

Spending time considering these things will make it more likely that your copy gets read. And since you spent all that time writing it, isn't that a good thing?

Type effects

Don't overdo it with the underlining, italics, bold, capitals and bullet points.

Old-fashioned American-style direct mail letters combined every type effect they could think of – and it looks bloody ugly and out of date. Underlining is particularly inelegant, whereas judicious use of italics can add a touch of class.

The simple rule is, the shorter the copy, the less you should need to use different type effects. And if you're capitalising words in a sentence, they should be small caps LIKE THIS, not full height caps that a) look like you're shouting and b) stand out too much from the rest of the copy. That's true for abbreviations like HSBC or TNT too. Not many people bother – probably because it's more effort to do in a word processing document – but it's the way to go.

Style

Fonts convey feeling and meaning. So the font you use can have an impact on your copy – choose a font that suits the tone and the feelings will be amplified.

Fonts are the clothes your words wear. So get to know them, see how they look at different sizes and styles and don't be afraid to mix a serif and sans-serif font in the same piece, provided they sit together well. Like Frutiger and Meridien, for example, which have a similar inner shape and proportion, and which were both designed by Mr Frutiger.

Dashes and hyphens

A tiny typographic point (or, rather, line) to finish on.

Dashes between phrases should be 'long dashes', known as 'em-space' dashes (because they are the length of the letter 'm' in the same font and size).

Type a dash on your keyboard and it first appears as an 'en-space' dash (ie the length of an 'n'). It may auto-correct to an em length dash when you then press the space-bar. See how the phrases 'auto-correct' and 'space-bar' are linked by hyphens (which are en-space in length), whereas phrases – like this one – are separated by dashes (which are em-space in length).

That's probably enough typography to contend with as a copywriter. Typography is a sophisticated, subtle art, but it's useful to have some basics to hand.

If you want to know more, an excellent book on typography (which I enjoyed so much I read it on a beach in Kefalonia) is Robert Brighurst's *The Elements of Typographic Style*.

iii. Layout

Like typography, layout is something whole books can be (and are) devoted to and it isn't something we need to spend too much time on.

But again, like typography, layout is something that affects the impact of your writing. Having a clear, unfussy layout that does justice to the copy is vital if it's to be read.

So, study some classic layouts and learn why they work. Don't let the design dominate the communication, have it serve the communication.

The classic press ad layout used to be one where the image was above the headline. On the basis that because people's eyes are drawn to images first, it made sense to let their eye go naturally from top to bottom, rather than have them look at the image, then have to look above it for the headline, then below it for the body copy.

I'm not saying all your layouts should be so strictly metered, just that it's useful to know the reason for choosing one layout over another. A couple of pointers for copy layout:

An ideal line length for body copy is 66 characters (including spaces).

If a line of copy from the left margin to the right (known as the 'measure') has considerably more or fewer characters than that, then your copy will be harder to read than it needs be.

That's for a single line. If you're writing something that will appear in columns, a little over 40 characters works well.

Paragraphs should (almost) never be more than five lines long, and should vary in length from single lines up to five.

Sentences should (almost) always be under 30 words long, and should vary in length (from one word to 30).

Indenting the first line of a paragraph tends to look rather old-fashioned nowadays. But maybe you're going for the traditional look. And the indents can make it easier to read.

A useful way to ensure good layouts is to save examples you think are strong. Tear them out of magazines, do screengrabs, take photos of them at tube stations.

Build up a folder of examples where the layout helps the copy tell the story, and use them for reference.

For more on layout, I recommend Jim Krause's *Index* book (or his set of three books, which also look at colour and design ideas) and *Basics Design 02: Layout* by Gavin Ambrose and Paul Harris.

1.3

How to write pleasingly

Aristotle, audience, tone & interest

i. Aristotle

Way back in Something BC, Aristotle (and others) devised a six point structure for successful rhetoric – a means of persuasion through oration. It goes:

1. Exordium (the introduction which catches the audience's attention)
2. Narratio (putting forward the relevant facts)
3. Divisio (revealing the issues to be proven)
4. Confirmatio (proving the case)
5. Confutatio (refuting any opposing case)
6. Peroratio (the summary which stirs the audience to action)

The (slightly) more modern iteration which you may well know is *AIDA*. An acronym which stands for Attention, Interest, Desire, Action and which is known as the 'purchase funnel'.

It's the idea that you should first get your audience's attention, then tell them something about your product / service that will interest them, create a desire for what you have to offer, then get them to take action.

And it's not a bad starting point. Even though brand campaigns, for example, might not have any *Action* in them. And you might not have separate, distinct sections of copy that are just about *Interest* or *Desire*.

Attention is important because – as I'm sure you know – you're not just competing with other ads (if you're doing an ad) in that product category. You're not even competing with every communication in that product category.

Nor are you even just competing with every advertising message your audience is likely to see that day.

You're competing with *everything* that's drawing their attention. The dog being sick. That red reminder from the phone company. A new drama on TV. A mild hangover. A major love interest.

Against that onslaught of demands, what chance have your carefully crafted words got? Not much, unless you can grab your audience's attention in the hint of a shaving of an iota of a scintilla of a soupçon of the nanosecond that they glance in the direction of your copy.

However. A word of caution.

Nowadays, people talk about *relevant abruption* or variations thereof. It's a qualified, more sophisticated version of the 'Attention' part of AIDA.

It means, get your audience's attention *in a way that's relevant* to them and your topic.

After all, you could just have the headline FREE MONEY. And that would probably get attention.

But if the communication isn't really about free money then you're not getting their attention in a relevant way. They'll read on long enough to realise you've misled them.

At that point they won't carry on reading, despite your best hopes. They'll turn away, annoyed. And, like the boy who cried wolf, you'll have tricked them to your own disadvantage: they'll be less likely to pay attention to you next time. Even if you then have something that would genuinely interest them.

So get your audience's attention with relevant abruption before drawing them in further... and arousing their desire. Doesn't that make copywriting sound sexy?

---

ii. Audience

In 2.2 of this book we'll take a closer look at the importance of knowing who you're writing for and how it should shape your copy.

But as a starting point, think about how you adjust your personality and behaviour according to who you're talking to 'in real life'.

While you're always 'you' with your own particular nature – your 'brand', let's say – you probably talk to your gran differently to how you talk to a friend. Which is different again to how you talk to your partner, which is different again to how you talk to your boss (unless you're sleeping with your boss, I suppose).

In the same way, you should write to suit the person it's for.

So a) know who you're writing to, b) put yourself in their shoes and c) write for them, in a style they will appreciate, with substance that will interest them.

a) Know who you're writing to

You may have seen marketing descriptions of an audience that look like this: 'ABC1 empty nesters who read *The Guardian* and like cookery programmes'.

Which means they're in socioeconomic group A or B or C1 (ie they're middle class white collar workers), their children have left home, they read a left-leaning broadsheet newspaper and they like Nigella. Now do you know who you're writing to?

Probably not. That kind of marketing jargon hardly puts a real person in your mind's eye.

What can be more useful is a 'pen portrait'. This describes the target audience a bit more fully with an invented example: a name, a picture and a description of what the target audience is actually like. A few paragraphs done in a 'Day in the life of' style, for instance.

At that point, think of someone you know who fits that profile.

b) Put yourself in their shoes

Think about the person you know and imagine you're them. Think about their likes and dislikes. Their views. The way they talk. What gets them nodding along, what interests them and what winds them up.

c) Write for them

Then write as if you're talking to them. More than that: as if you're trying to persuade them. Of course, any communication or wider campaign is usually targeted so that the person you're writing to is the person most likely to be interested in your product / service / offer anyway, so it shouldn't be a huge stretch.

But it does help to ensure you're writing for the audience, rather than for yourself or even the client.

Handy hint

Always write as if you're talking to an individual, rather than a group. So don't say "We hope everyone will…", say "We hope you will…". Don't say "People like you…", say "You…" Don't say "Cyclists often find…", say "As a cyclist, you may find…" Talk to someone as a singular entity, not part of an amorphous mass.

iii. Tone

Everyone's copy has a tone of voice. And it's rarely the voice they speak with. In fact, it's often a voice *no-one* would speak with.

Perhaps you know someone with what used to be called a 'telephone manner'.

They talk normally until they're introduced to someone they've never met before. And suddenly they're all, "Oh, hel-low, how orfully dee-lightful to meeeet you, reeeelly sow ek-citing." They try to sound all educated, like what Mrs Malaprop did.

People often adopt their own special tone of voice in copy too.

Instead of trying to write the way they'd speak, they write in an affected, trying-too-hard and pseudo-clever way.

Don't be one of those people.

When you've written a draft, read your copy out loud. And really listen to what you're saying. Does it sound natural and conversational? If not, make it so. Better yet, get someone else to read it out loud to you – because then you'll see if they read it with the rhythm, inflection and meaning you intended.

Handy hint

Write in a friendly, easy style. Always look for the shorter, simpler word. Look for words with fewer syllables. Look for words which are more 'concrete' (rather than abstract) and more common (Anglo Saxon than Latin).

In part 3, the *Quick tips* section, we'll look at how the occasional unusual word can work well, but that's the *occasional* word. The other 99% should be the easiest to read you can find. Don't turn your copy into a Will Self novel – brilliantly written, but some of us need an accompanying dictionary to follow it.

Of course, tone of voice is about more than just being natural and conversational; it also conveys personality. Earlier when talking about the *universal objective*, we looked at balancing style and substance. Well, it's often the personality you write with that leads the style.

One way to write with a particular tone of voice is to think of someone you know, or a famous person whose voice you can call to mind (or watch clips of on YouTube) to imitate.

Once I had to write a letter that was being signed by Lady Thatcher. So not only was I writing about her life and experiences, I was writing it in her voice, too. One sentence was:

"And on the 4th May, 1979, I became your Prime Minister."

If I'd been writing it in my tone of voice, I'd have said "And in 1979 I became Prime Minister." I wouldn't have put the specific day, but I thought she would be very particular about it.

I wouldn't have said "your Prime Minister" either. I'd have been squeamish about saying "your", worrying it sounded rather self-important and assumptive (especially as not everyone voted Conservative). But again, I thought it was the kind of language she would use.

On reflection, maybe I should have said "And on the 4th May, 1979, We became your Prime Minister." The 'Iron Lady' was fond of using 'The royal we'.

So you can create a tone by imagining a person. Or you could keep in mind an adjective which best summarises the tone you believe would be most effective. Here are a dozen examples:

1. Authoritative
2. Jokey
3. Witty
4. Hushed
5. Conspiratorial
6. Excited
7. Positive
8. Angry
9. Seductive
10. Worried
11. Reassuring
12. Mysterious

There are many more of course, but if you are considering developing a tone in that way, check with the client to see if they agree. One challenge you may find is that while your client may agree that yes, the copy should aim for (for instance) a *witty* tone, they may not agree that your copy has successfully achieved it.

Tone of voice is critical, and we'll come back to it in Part 2 of this book.

But the most important point I want to get across here is to be wary of tone. If in doubt, aim for a fairly *neutral* tone.

Certainly, be very wary of trying to imbue your copy with a *great deal* of tone – firstly, it's hard to do well, secondly it can overwhelm the content and thirdly, it can be misinterpreted. That's because a) you're not able to judge the audience's reaction to see if they like your tone and b) the written word makes tone more ambiguous than the spoken word.

"And of course, who wouldn't want to spend the day exploring the nearby Pencil museum?" If that was spoken, you'd be able to tell that the speaker was being sarcastic. Written, who knows. Maybe they find pencils fascinating. (It's in Keswick, Cumbria, if you're a big fan of pencils.)

For example

So generally, your tone should be fairly neutral, with (usually) a gentle feeling of being warm, conversational and approachable. Less is more.

iv. Interest

To write pleasingly, you need to keep your audience interested. The easy way to do that, of course, is to write about a subject which interests your audience.

Once again, what you're writing about is the most important thing. After that, the way you're writing can add further interest.

Look at the contents listing for this part of the book.

Its title is *The Fantastic Four.* Another section is *The Famous Five* and another is *The Magnificent Seven.* All book / film titles with a number in, and the number goes up each time.

Every chapter in this *Fantastic Four* section alliterates: purposefully, practically, pleasingly, persuasively.

And finally, each of these four chapters has four sub-sections, creating balance and symmetry.

I realise that telling you that is far from interesting. But it does make the list of contents a little more interesting… without being at the expense of the contents.

There are thousands of ways in which you can make your copy a little more interesting, but here's something that doesn't: an avalanche of adjectives and adverbs.

Sometimes people think that to make their writing more interesting, they should smother every sentence with descriptive adjectives and adverbs. Actually, it makes your writing sound like bad romantic fiction. Ruthlessly edit out these modifiers and you'll often end up with much stronger, punchier copy.

In Part 2 we'll be looking at writing that's bewitchingly engaging right from the start. But, since we're already starting to look at what's interesting, here are seven techniques you can weave into your copy to give it a little more pizzazz:

1) Big bang

Hit the ground running. Think of your copy as an action movie that starts with a huge explosion which makes the audience go 'Woah'. That means an approach which doesn't build up to the subject: it opens with something as dramatic and attention-grabbing as possible.

2) Anecdotes

A moment ago I was talking about tone, and I gave the example of the time I wrote as Lady Thatcher. An anecdote which, I hope, made explaining tone more interesting.

After dinner speakers: most of their act is a collection of anecdotes. In fact, an anecdote lifts almost any presentation; it gives it colour and personality. And it's the same for your copy.

Some anecdotes can be about your own experiences. Others can just be stories from anywhere – anything that helps illustrate your subject.

I once wrote a piece that was about honesty. In it, I related an anecdote about Koko, the famous gorilla. What's she famous for? Well, Koko, a lowlands gorilla who lives at San Francisco zoo, is fluent in sign language. And she can understand around 2,000 words of spoken English.

She also has a pet cat, given to her when it was just a kitten.

One day, Koko's keepers heard a terrible commotion coming from Koko's enclosure. They went to investigate, and saw that the sink had been ripped off the wall in a tantrum.

They scolded Koko for her fit of pique. At which point Koko pointed at her tiny little kitten and signed that no, it wasn't Koko who had broken the sink… it was the kitten.

For example

So there you go; an anecdote about a fibbing gorilla that made a piece about honesty more interesting.

3) Water cooler moment

This is the idea that people at work, all gathered around the water cooler first thing in the morning, talk about whatever's on their mind – whatever's grabbed their interest.

It may be last night's football game or episode of EastEnders. Or, if there's a big story in the news, it might be something to do with that story which they think other people might not have heard. Something that might impress or interest them.

Because one of the reasons people like interesting snippets is so they can pass them on, and seem interesting by association. Which means facts can be interesting.

Did you know that Wembley Stadium has more toilets than any other building in the world? (2,618 apparently.)

For example

Water cooler moments can include:

- Facts
- Statistics
- Revelations
- Gossip
- Clever solutions
- News
- Controversy

Basically, giving your audience a new, bite-size, soundbite of knowledge they can either personally make use of or pass on to someone else. It will always help make your copy more interesting and better appreciated.

4) Wordplay

I pointed out that the titles of the copy sections in this book are from films / books with a number in the title. And that the chapters within this section all alliterate. They're minor flourishes and many people might not even notice them. But for those that do, they add a little rhythm and interest to an otherwise pretty dull list.

As with tone, wordplay is one of those things that needs experience to do well – beginners tend to do it too much and too clumsily. It needs a light touch, to complement what you're saying, rather than become what you're saying.

I've seen a lot of work from junior copywriters where I ended up crossing out most of the wordplay (to their frustration), because it was unnecessary and distracting.

We'll look at a more comprehensive list of 20 wordplay devices in 3.7 of this book.

5) It's all about you

Use 'you'. Yep, it's as easy as that. But simple as it is, basic as it is, look for it in everything you write. People are interested in themselves and using 'you' reminds them that your topic is really all about them.

You can see how often I use it throughout this book. In fact, I always go back through my copy to make sure I've used 'you' enough.

When you've written your first draft, check where the first occurrence of 'you' is. If it's too low down, so the copy doesn't sound like it's 'all about you', then consider sticking one in earlier. Even if that means contriving a new sentence that only exists to get the word 'you' in.

Of course, some styles / subjects won't have a single 'you' in the copy. But most copy benefits from bringing the audience into it.

6) Back to the start

A simple copy device you see commonly in press ads, direct mail letters and magazine interviews: the copy begins with a certain concept before moving onto the main topic.

Then at the end, the opening gambit is reprised. It 'closes the circle' and just feels 'neat' for the reader. It ties everything up in a nice creative bow and makes it a little more interesting.

A blog I wrote began 'When my mum was a girl, not many young people had watches. They were a bit of a status symbol. So in the summer, she and her friends would stick a watch paper template around their wrists. Which would give them a watch tan line – so it looked like you had a watch, you just didn't happen to be wearing it.'

Then it moved on to the main topic (about the difference between motivation and behaviour) without any further mention of watches until the very end: 'It's why understanding motivation, not just measuring behaviour, can be so important. And why people no longer buy watches to tell the time. But to tell you something about them.'

7) Quotable

Quotes always add interest, and they don't need to be from someone the reader has heard of.

Simply because they're speech, they're direct from a real person, not a hidden writer, so they add gravitas to your words. They also add a different tone of voice to that of the rest of the copy. They can endorse what the rest of the copy is saying (effectively you're writing something that's just agreeing with itself, yet somehow that works).

And it also means you can get away saying things that otherwise, you couldn't say.

For example

I've seen a skincare TV ad featuring a minor celebrity. At the end of the ad, she says, "For me, it's the best moisturiser there is." Of course, the company couldn't say it was the best moisturiser there is, that would be untrue or unprovable. But the celeb can say that, 'in their opinion', it is the best. And this ringing endorsement makes the whole story a little more interesting.

Let's refocus for a moment. Why we doing all this?

To entertain? To inform? To make an announcement? Because we've got some marketing budget to spend?

We may be doing a little of all of those, but only in order to achieve the real goal: to *persuade*. Never forget that – because other people involved in the project might.

Your copy must persuade someone to do something that they would not do otherwise. Your copy must change behaviour. Your copy must *sell*.

WIIFM, Maslow, motivation & emotional vs rational

Good copy is written salesmanship. You're trying to sell something to someone you haven't even met. And you can only do it with the power of the written word.

That's not easy – which is perhaps why some people forget that's the real purpose of good copy. They settle for copy that's merely informative or entertaining or client-pleasing or brand-building or awareness-raising and hope that the reader will just 'buy'.

But they won't. Not unless we sell. Here's how.

---

i. WIIFM

A phrase you may already know: 'What's In It For Me?'

Just imagine (since it's likely to be true) that if your target audience does happen to glance briefly in the direction of your copy, that's what they'll be thinking. *What's in it for me?*

You've got to answer that question.

At the beginning, in the middle, at the end. And everywhere in between.

It means, when gathering your *substance,* don't think about what interests you; think only about what's going to interest the audience. And what will most interest the audience is what's going to make their life better. What will benefit them in some way. And the bigger the benefit, the more they'll be interested.

Let's look at three ways of answering an audience's cry of *What's in it for me.*

ii. Maslow

Maslow was a psychologist who, in 1943, categorised the basic needs of humans and put them in an order. With the most fundamental needs at the bottom of a pyramid, and the most esoteric needs further up. He called it a *Hierarchy of Needs*.

The idea is that only when people have satisfied their needs on one level will they start worrying about the needs on the next level up.

There are lots of versions of his pyramid, but most look like this:

Why is this important?

Well, it's important to know (and tell your audience) which of these needs will be met by your product / service / offer / brand.

It's also useful because sometimes you may be helping your audience to meet more than one need on the pyramid – in which case, lead with the need that's lower down. Gather your content around that need, because it's more fundamental and therefore more persuasive.

Say you're doing something for a charity. Oxfam maybe. An appeal to help the people of Sudan, who are in desperate need of clean, safe water.

Clean water is right at the base of Maslow's pyramid. People know it's a fundamental need. It's likely, therefore, to be a more powerful, persuasive story than talking about helping people in Sudan who've been separated from their family to find them again. That's from the 'love / belonging' level – higher up and therefore less powerful.

So focus your communication on the lack of water, not the family separation.

At the same time, the Hierarchy of Needs can also give you a steer on how to answer the reader's question 'What's in it for me?' – even for a charity appeal.

Which might surprise you, since in a charity appeal you're asking people to make a donation for which they (in theory) get nothing back. It's not *their* physiological needs which are being met after all, it's someone else's – someone they don't even know.

What is in it for the audience is a boost to their self-esteem.

That's why charity appeals should make it clear how much the audience is appreciated, how wonderful they are. The audience can meet a self-actualisation need (morality and personal fulfilment) if we tell them just what a fantastic difference their support is going to make (and clearly show them how).

And that's really useful, because it means you can get both a physiological need for the people of Sudan *and* a self-actualisation need for the audience into your copy.

Now. Maslow's theory has been around for a long time and is widely used, but it's not always helpful.

For instance, if you're doing a TV ad for McDonalds, where does that sit on Maslow?

You're advertising food – does that mean you're meeting a physiological need? Well, fast food is eaten for convenience and pleasure, not because you'll starve otherwise.

So actually, McDonalds advertising in Maslow terms might be more about belonging or self-esteem. But writing an ad for a Big Mac around those themes might not lead to very effective work. Luckily, there are two other ways to look at WIIFM – motivations and emotional vs rational.

iii. Motivations

If Maslow is about needs, we could also look at universal human *wants*. It might include, in no particular order, these 32 motivations:

1.	to be liked	17.	to be happy
2.	to be loved	18.	to have fun
3.	to be popular	19.	to gain knowledge
4.	to be appreciated /valued	20.	to be healthy
5.	to be right	21.	to satisfy curiosity
6.	to feel important	22.	for convenience
7.	to make money	23.	out of fear
8.	to save money	24.	out of greed
9.	to save time	25.	out of guilt
10.	to make work easier	26.	to belong
11.	to be secure	27.	to gain respect
12.	to be attractive	28.	to avoid pain
13.	to be sexy	29.	to get pleasure
14.	to be comfortable	30.	to give life meaning
15.	to stand out	31.	to achieve something
16.	to fit in	32.	to win

How can your copy promise people one or more of these things?

How will reading what you've written make them 'rich and famous', for example?

Back to the McDonald's TV ad. Now that we're not looking at a Maslow need, we might look at number 29 from the list of motivations: pleasure (the taste) as the thing we will promote in our ad. Or even number 17: because it makes you happy.

Don't underestimate this stuff. It's incredibly powerful because it's what people – your audience – *want*.

Your audience isn't interested in hearing about the heritage of a company, how it's been going for over 50 years, how the company is committed to this or passionate about that, blah blah blah. And they're not interested in how you've tried to make your copy more richly descriptive than a Tolkien novel. They just want to know: What's In It For Me?

This list of motivations works in every medium for every audience and regardless of whatever trends are happening. Why? Because these are things that have motivated humans for thousands of years.

We might believe we're all very sophisticated and media-savvy, but the basic blood-and-guts motivators are in our DNA, in our evolution, and they haven't changed.

It's why those spam emails continue to draw people in.

The Nigerian princess who promises you millions of dollars if you give her your bank account details. The get-rich-quick business ventures which claim 'I'm making $15,000 a week online, just by working a few hours doing something I enjoy!' The Viagra emails that say – and I quote – D'UWantTtoHavePpefe rctSexAllNightIonng?

They all play on promising people something they want. A motivation they want to fulfil so badly, they're prepared to suspend their better judgement. Even though it's telling them that if an offer sounds too good to be true, it probably is.

iv. Emotional vs rational

It's said that people buy cars for emotional reasons, but justify them for rational ones.

Something that people who make car ads know all too well.

If you buy a new car, you'll *actually* be driving it in rush hour on the M6 in pouring rain and realising that the windscreen wipers are a bit ropey. But in the ad, they show you the car winding through a glorious mountain pass in the South of France, with not a single other car in sight. Something you'll probably never do.

And they tell you almost nothing about the specifics of the car – even though it's likely to be the second most expensive purchase you'll ever make.

They just focus on associating the car with positive emotions: joy, freedom, excitement, sense of achievement, feeling special. And it works.In fact, it's often been found that emotional reasons to do something are much more persuasive than rational ones.

Let me say that again, because it can be something of a revelation: *emotional persuaders are usually more potent than rational ones.*

The reason it's a revelation is, in our modern high-tech world of science and research and sophisticated media-savvy consumers, we've come to believe that we're rational creatures.

That logic is best and reason always wins.

And everyone likes to think they make decisions logically, not emotionally.

But it's not true.

So: make sure your copy has emotional and rational persuaders in it. And don't *say* the emotions, make your audience *feel* them.

It's a subject that deserves a lot more exploration – and we'll return to emotion and persuasion in the *Compel* section of Part 2 of this book.

But for now, whether you're writing copy or just reviewing it, always check it against a list of the biggest rational benefits and the biggest emotional benefits you've got – and make sure *both* are in there.

In summary

Here we are then. At the end of our introductory tour of the copywriting fairground. We've had some candy floss, we've been on the dodgems and we've felt a bit sick on the waltzers. We've even won a small cuddly toy on the rifle range.

Or, to lose the metaphor: we've covered the four fundamentals of decent copy.

They alone won't give you breathtaking, groundbreaking, award-winning copy. But they will mean communications that are clear, focused, interesting and effective. They'll make your copy righter.

Before we move on, here's a reminder of what *not* to do – ten common copy clangers we've covered in this section:

1. Thinking a complex product / service / idea needs a complex explanation
2. Writing about too many things at once
3. Starting slowly and continuing vaguely
4. Writing to impress, rather than to communicate
5. Writing for yourself, not the audience
6. Writing to lots of people, not just one
7. Writing copy with too much tone / too little tone
8. Being boring
9. Being only rational and forgetting the emotion
10. Being just informative or entertaining, rather than persuasive.

Okay. Now we're ready to get into the really juicy stuff. The advanced *Famous Five* that reveal how to write great copy from scratch.

We'll look at some examples, take in brands, media, concepts, linguistic mastery and how to be more persuasive than that silver-tongued serpent from The Garden of Eden.

2

The Famous Five:
How to write great copy

Whoa, hold on.

Go back a second and read that list once more. One to five.

Because that's it. The sequence that gets you from zero to hero.

It's the five-step system any copywriter worth his sodium chloride will go through (whether consciously or not, whether in that exact sequence or not) to get great copy.

Content and *Context* are the 'before'.

Because as they say in the army, 'Proper planning prevents piss poor performance'.

Create and *Compel* are the 'during'.

They're where rigorous technical understanding meets creative flair and personality. So your copy says the right thing to the right person in the right way. Writing that's engaging to read, easy to absorb… while surreptitiously bending the reader to your will.

Craft is the 'after'.

Reviewing, editing, honing. Some people hate editing because it can mean cutting away their favourite lines. For others it's the best bit, polishing a lump of raw copy into a glistening jewel.

Either way, spending time on the 'after' can lift the quality of your work considerably.

You may not do them as linearly as this. You might take these five steps (or aspects of them) in a different order. You may do several at once. In truth, you may do a bit of one, move on to another and then go back.

Either way, in my experience you might spend around 30% of your time in preparation and planning, 40% actually writing your first draft and 30% honing and refining it.

So. We'll start with a crisp sheet of A4 and a Mont Blanc Starwalker. Or a laptop screen and a winking cursor. Or if you want to be old-school about it, a bookie's pen and the back of a fag packet.

And from nothing but the same words everyone else has to play with, write *great* copy. We'll start by asking the most important question of all:

What the hell are you trying to say?

i. Proposition

Proposition,
interrogation
& insight

It's often said that 'What you say is more important than
the way you say it'.

That's not always true of course. A great orator with mediocre
content can often convince people more effectively than a poor
speaker with great content.

Just as a rubbish singer with a lot of enthusiasm can be
a more entertaining karaoke star than a half-decent singer
with no personality.

In fact, in advertising and marketing – a world of me-too
products and services where we're often selling the same thing
to the same person using the same media – the *way* we tell
the story may be the *only* point of difference.

But in most circumstances, *what* you say is generally regarded
as the biggie.

Content is king. And the starting point for that is the proposition.
If you've a strong, clear proposition then your screen's cursor
is going to wink at you chummily, not mockingly. For every
communication you need to know: if our target audience only
remembers one thing, what should that one thing be?

That's the proposition.

A proposition is the single-minded, single most important
message we want our communication to convey. More
colloquially, you could call it 'the elevator pitch'.

Imagine your perfect customer steps into a lift at the same
time you do. But they're getting out in a couple of floors.
So you've got eight seconds to tell them why they should
buy what you're selling.

How to come up with a strong proposition.

1) Look at your specific objective (explored in 1.1 of this book).
2) Look at the key insights you've uncovered / been given.
3) Look at the key benefit / advantage / compelling idea of
   your subject. Then:

4) Bring those elements together into a single-minded sentence that tells the audience the most compelling, persuasive thing they could ever hear about your subject.

For example

Say you're writing an ad for one of the big tour operators. One that does Balinese package holidays, which have been popular with honeymooners.

Trouble is, newlyweds are a fairly small audience. So you've got a declining market.

Your objective is simple: persuade more people to go, not just young couples who've recently tied the knot. People in their forties and fifties (who often have a higher disposable income) would be ideal. They're people who enjoy great beaches too, but they also value high standards of service.

So… since it's a great honeymoon destination but you want to entice couples in their forties / fifties, why not position it as a great place to enjoy a second honeymoon?

And your proposition becomes:

Enjoy a second honeymoon even more memorable than your first – with a holiday in beautiful Bali where every day is a special occasion and every guest is treated like royalty.

It's not a headline, strapline, slogan or whatever else you want to call it.

It's a blunt form of words that will probably never appear like that anywhere in the ad. But it is, in effect, what you'd want someone to say the ad was about, if they read it. It's the 'take out' you want them to go away with.

In fact, if your audience can tell you what the proposition is even though it isn't written explicitly in those words in your copy, then you know what you've done is on brief.

And that, my friend, is what success looks like.

A second, simple way of arriving at the proposition is to consider all the information from a problem / solution perspective. What is the 'problem' your audience has? What is the solution to that problem which your product / service can provide? State your proposition in those terms.

For the Bali ad, we might say the problem for our audience is that holidays have lost their romance. Their magic. Bali, a 'second honeymoon' destination, is the solution to that. And that problem / solution dynamic gives us a clear way to express the proposition.

But like I say, write your proposition bluntly. Without embellishment.

Sometimes people have an urge to write them as if they were a slogan. I saw one the other day: 'Expect the unexpected'. It was for a bank account. Yet the core benefit / solution of the account wasn't that it was 'constantly surprising'. Yes, the audience might be surprised by the benefits, but it doesn't tell them what those benefits *are*, which is much more important.

An offer is not a benefit.

Ok, an offer is a benefit. But, it's not the main benefit of the product or service – it's an extra incentive *on top of* the main benefits. So under most circumstances you shouldn't lead with it.

For instance, in the case of the Bali holiday maybe the client was offering a superior room for the price of a standard room. That's great: it's an incentive to book now, while the offer is available. But it's not the headline message – it's not as compelling as the idea of Bali being the place to enjoy a second honeymoon.

The offer is an extra little push to get your audience to 'act now' once they've been won over by your core proposition.

In fact, that's why offers and incentives are often time-limited or only available to a certain number of customers (or not even guaranteed for everyone, like a prize). They're there to create a sense of urgency to compel people to take your recommended course of action.

"This job's much too complicated to summarise in a sentence."

If someone else is writing the proposition, they may argue that the story can't be boiled down into a single, pithy sentence. That there's not one important message – there are eight, all of equal importance.

Well, tell them that the audience may only remember one thing – so it's better we decide what that one thing should be rather than leave it to chance.

It's said that an editor of *The Sun* wouldn't let any story run unless the journalist could express that story in 20 words or less. Using vocabulary a nine year-old could understand.

See for yourself: have a look at today's front page story of *The Sun*. Look at the headline, the subhead and the first sentence.

The headline tells you something. The subhead tells you the same thing again, just using different words and adding a bit of detail. And the first sentence tells you again, adding a little bit more detail yet.

That first sentence summarises the whole story that's then told fully in the rest of the article. And the first sentence is usually 20 words or less.

For example

Here's one of their most famous, about the sinking of the Belgrano. Headline: GOTCHA. Subhead: Our lads sink gun boat and hole cruiser. First sentence: The Navy had the Argies on their knees last night after a devastating double punch.

If *The Sun* can summarise any world event in 20 words or less, the story you want to tell can probably be expressed as pithily too. I'm not as strict as the editor of *The Sun* was, I reckon a good proposition can be up to 30 words long (like the Bali one above).

But that essence, that pure distillation of your whole communication is what you're looking for.

Handy hint

Once you know your proposition, the one thing your audience must remember, write it out with a thick black Sharpie and stick it somewhere prominent.

It's easy to get into the flow of your writing and wander off topic, or write something that's almost on brief… but not quite. Having the proposition staring you in the face as you work helps make sure that doesn't happen.

ii. Interrogation

You've got a proposition. Now comes the *Marmite* bit: the research.

Some people love doing research, some people hate it. Both have their pitfalls. If you just rely on what's in the brief, you're likely to end up with a generic blandathon.

But if you do too much research, you'll get lost in minutiae and end up with lots of obscure stuff. Then you'll tie yourself in knots trying to choose what to include and what to leave out.

Instead, interrogate the subject and find out as much as you can *in the time you have*. Writing copy means learning lots of little things about a huge range of subjects. You become a superficial expert in dozens of different areas.

So keep digging until you find something that most of your audience won't know.

Something interesting, factual, surprising, shocking or illuminating.

If the proposition is 'The elevator pitch', here you're looking for 'The water cooler' moment – some little nugget that you could imagine people sharing when they bump into each other at the office water cooler. Some 'Did you know' tidbit.

I've seen plenty of work where the copywriter hadn't bothered to find out anything more than was on the brief. And since people often don't find out much to put in the brief, the result... doesn't add up to much.

As the old saying goes 'You can't bore people into buying your product'.

If there's a detail the client hasn't provided, but you think would be useful, write it in the copy. Put 'Bought by more than X,000 customers in the UK every year' for instance, so the client knows to get hold of the figure for you. It's better to show them what you need than just leave it out.

Handy hint

Your content needs to be rich and inviting: lean, because there's nothing that doesn't add to the story, but sprinkled with the kind of detail that makes it more interesting and authentic.

When writing an appeal for Oxfam and talking about a lack of clean, safe water in Sudan, find out a little about the subject. Discover that the women there have to walk for three hours to collect water from a stagnant pond because it's the only water available.

Discover that they have to walk in 43 degree heat. That they do so knowing they'll have to make the trip twice more that day, carrying an earthenware pot of water on their heads that weighs more than a packed suitcase. And discover that swarms of mosquitoes are drawn to the stagnant water to breed, so on every trip the women risk deadly malaria, for which they have no medicine.

Now, instead of talking in general terms about the need for 'clean, safe water', you can really paint a picture of what it's like for a woman in Sudan. You can get your audience to imagine waking up and setting off on their first dangerous, exhausting three hour trip of the day, taking weary step after weary step across the desolate sands known as 'goz' in baking, unrelenting heat – just to collect enough water to prepare breakfast for their children.

Find out more about the subject. Get hold of everything else the client's ever had written.

Get on the internet and don't stop at Wikipedia or the client's homepage: keep digging until you unearth something more interesting. Something your audience won't know. Something perhaps your client won't even know.

Collect up the nuggets you find in a little folder (electronic or physical) somewhere. These little gems are going to make your copy sparkle.

There's a second, rather wonderful way of interrogating the subject to come up with new, interesting nuggets about it, of course. And that's to use it / experience it / investigate it yourself.

In the case of the Bali holidays we looked at earlier, you'd go on a holiday to Bali (not too much of a hardship) and you'd get tons of rich material. Your holiday journal would capture great moments that you'd probably never unearth any other way.

And by later reliving some of those moments in your copy, you'd create a much more authentic, compelling story.

Or here's a more prosaic example: say you're writing web copy for the Banana Guard by Aberrant Designs. You know this thing? A yellow, plastic, hinged container for putting bananas in.

You could find out what it's for from their website. Or you could buy one, use it and see what occurs to you. Or you could just 'interrogate the product' – play with it, examine it and imagine what all the benefits of it could be.

The main benefit it's promoted for is protecting your banana from being bashed around in your bag. I bought one not to protect the banana, but my bag – after a forgotten banana dissolved in a previous bag, ruining it.

So that's a second, complementary benefit for a start. Here's a longer list:

1. Protects your banana from damage
2. Protects your bag or clothes from banana stains
3. Works on virtually any size / shape banana (fits 95%)
4. Holds the skin afterwards if you've nowhere to put it
5. Holes keep fruit fresh (ventilation prevents premature ripening)
6. Bright so it's easy to find
7. Looks like a piece of banana art and looks good in fruit bowl
8. Acts as a visual reminder to get one of your five a day
9. Can hang it up by one of the holes so it's out the way (eg off your desk)
10. Lasts a lifetime (approx. 6,000 bananas), and at £6 that's 0.1p per banana!
11. Stops other fruit from over-ripening by being close to banana
12. Also works with some cucumbers, celery sticks, carrot...

13. Subtle branding keeps it classy (but reminds you of name in case people ask)

14. Unlike most kitchen products, no sticker that's impossible to get off properly

15. Can be used stuck in a pocket as a pretend gun

16. Light: only two ounces makes it easy to carry around

17. Compact: takes up little more space than a banana, so fits neatly in a handbag or suitcase

18. Makes you look wise and healthy

19. Encourages people to eat more bananas because they're no longer worried about carrying them: studies show people with a Banana Guard eat 18% more bananas than they did before

20. Dishwasher-proof so easy to clean

21. Comes in different colours: how about a blue banana! Or a green one!

22. Has some friends: the Pear guard and the Froot case so you can collect the whole set

23. Made from FDA approved recyclable plastic so they're environmentally friendly

Et voila: you have a longer list of benefits and more interesting things to say.

Benefit 19 – that people with a Banana Guard eat 18% more bananas – is made up; it's an example of what I mentioned earlier, 'Wouldn't it be great if we could say…' Then it's just a matter of talking to the client to see if any studies do exist, or if there's any data they could find out.

If not, maybe they'd like to do some research into it, because it'd be a great selling point.

iii. Insight

"Eureka," said Archimedes upon spilling bathwater and Radox all over his travertine.

That moment – when you turn a fact, idea or bit of knowledge into something you can use – that's an insight.

To put it another way, if your proposition is *what* you're talking about, the insight may be *why* you're talking about it.

Many strong insights are *audience* insights – something you've discovered about the audience that helps show why your subject is exactly what they should be interested in.

I say 'discovered' – many insights you can find out by reading the research or information gathering or examining the data or holding a co-creation session. But many of the best insights are intuitive.

In Schipol airport in Holland, for instance, they wanted to get men to improve their aim at the urinals. They couldn't really run a focus group, asking men about their peeing habits. Nor could they stand in the men's toilets with a clipboard, observing what went on.

They had to use intuition into what men are like to come up with an insight into what would work.

What they did was engrave a fly on the urinal. Near the plughole.

And men suddenly had something to aim at. Misfires went down by 80%. Which saved on cleaning costs and made the toilets nicer.

Because someone had the insight that if men saw a fly, they'd aim for it.

You may not have been provided with a neatly packaged insight with your brief. But that doesn't mean you can't get one, by really putting yourself in your audience's shoes and considering how they think, feel and act.

Use what you do know about them to take that next step: something you don't know for sure, but which your intuition tells you might well be the case.

And see if that gives you a great angle for positioning your subject.

When copywriter Alec Brownstein wanted a job at a big agency in New York, his intuited insight was that creative directors in New York were probably very vain (unlike us modest ones in England). He thought they were probably so vain they googled their own names on a regular basis.

So he used Google Adwords. And when any one of New York's five most prominent CDs googled their own names, his one line ad (saying it was fun to google your own name and also fun to hire him), appeared above the search results. Four of the CDs ended up interviewing him. Two of them offered him a job. He took one of them.

His ad had cost $6.

Let's go back to the Banana Guard: we have the list of product benefits from our interrogation session earlier. Benefit 4 is: gives you somewhere to put the skin afterwards.

Why would that be useful? Only when you're somewhere where there isn't a bin handy. Maybe when you're in the car (as a passenger, of course. It's probably illegal to drive and eat a banana at the same time. Unless you use your knees to steer, in which case I'm sure it's okay.)

So there's a bit of intuitive insight: we can use Benefit 4 as a reason to appeal to people who travel in cars (ie, an awful lot of people). Have a Banana Guard handy and you can take fruit in the car and have somewhere to put the skin afterwards, without leaving it to rot in the ashtray or naughtily throwing it out of the window.

In fact, that insight might then be a recommendation for the company to sell the Banana Guard at petrol stations / motorway services, with Benefit 4 clearly flagged on the tag.

Brand,
audience
& medium

When you have the *Content*, the next step is to get a good feel for the *Context* in which your copy will appear.

So remember BAM. *Brand. Audience. Medium.* The three corners of a Context Pyramid, if you will – and three elements which should shape the way you bring the proposition to life.

Each is a vast and important subject in its own right. But we're just going to touch on how you might start to consider each area and how they might influence your copy.

After that, experience and endeavour will tell you all you need to know about them. That and the recommended reading I'll suggest along the way.

However. A word of warning.

There's an awful lot of rubbish talked about brands, audiences and media. There are hundreds of would-be gurus on the seminar circuit, selling their time on the idea that they can impart vital wisdom. About 'How to talk to baby boomers'. 'Engaging the grey market'. 'Why TV is dead'. 'Building your brand through Twitter'. 'How Social Media Has Totally Made Everything Else Like Soooo Lame'.

It's in the best interests of these experts to make things seem more complicated than they really are. Because if it was simple, they'd have nothing to talk about on the lecture circuit.

Nothing to get prospective clients panicking about, paying to hear more for fear of being left behind.

The truth is, yes, audiences do change. A bit.

And technology changes at a phenomenal pace, bringing new ways to reach people and new ways to embellish your message.

But behind it all, human beings have changed very little. For millennia.

We're still motivated by the same things we always were. We process information with eyes and ears and brains that haven't changed one iota in generations. We still have the same range of emotions.

And happily for copywriters, we're still influenced by the way someone uses language.

i. Brand

When I was a young wordsmith, books on copywriting didn't even mention brands. They were old-school guides to writing hard-sell copy, littered with exclamation marks and talk of 'coupons'.

Trouble is, they taught you to make every piece of copy sound identical.

Today, a company's brand may be one of its most valuable assets. Coca Cola's brand, for example, is valued at well over 60 billion dollars.

Now, they stopped having cocaine in Coke (about 9 milligrams a glass, allegedly) way back in 1903. And without the marching powder, what's Coke? Just burpy brown sugar water. At least, it would be, if it didn't have 60 billion dollars' worth of brand equity behind it.

So if you're writing for Coke, you need to get the brand right, to avoid damaging that 60 billion dollar asset. But how do you write copy that's brand literate?

Firstly, let me say that brand, tone of voice and visual identity are terms that are often used quite interchangeably. I'm going to distinguish between them.

A visual identity is *not* a company's brand. The visual identity (logo, colours, fonts, the way they do layouts, use images etc) is what helps the audience recognise that the communication is *from* that brand.

Which should start to get the audience thinking and feeling everything associated with that brand.

Tone of voice could be called the personality that the brand's communications speak with.

However, I've seen 'brand bibles' from all sorts companies that all have very similar descriptions of their tone of voice, despite being very different brands.

The tone of voice guide will say things like 'trustworthy', 'straightforward', 'approachable', 'authoritative' and so on. Your tone of voice is trustworthy? As opposed to your competitors, who are going for what, untrustworthy?

Meanwhile, style guides that tell you how to use the brand's tone of voice are often little more than basic guides to good English usage. I've seen many that were just ripped-off from *The Guardian's* style guide (which, incidentally, is a very useful resource – find it online).

Because of that, it's often best to look at the overall *brand positioning* – the biggie that sits above both tone of voice and visual identity.

There are lots of definitions of what a brand is – I'll just say it's the 'take out' that the audience has from coming into contact with the company. Let me repeat that: the *take out*. What the audience actually thinks, feels and experiences. Which is not necessarily what the company is trying to project.

And *contact* means any possible way they might 'brush with the brand' – seeing the advertising, owning the product, phoning customer services, meeting someone in a bar who works at the company.

So: what are the brand values? What's its personality? What feelings does it want to conjure in its audience?

You could think of the brand as the 'complementary product' you get when you buy the actual product.

Handy hint

So if you buy Levi's jeans, you're getting a pair of denim trousers… but the complementary product you're getting is the Levi's brand: everything that little red tag represents. (Which, I guess, Levi's would hope is the idea of being a bit cool. Knowing your denim and buying from a brand that has a greater denim heritage than other premium-priced jean makers.)

That's quite useful for copy. Because the feelings your copy engenders can be the 'complementary product' people are buying.

Innocent smoothies are a fantastic example of this – and yes, they've been used as an example of a strong brand in 90% of brand discussions for years now. But copy is an area where they're particularly strong.

Whizzed-up fruit in a (recycled) plastic bottle. That's what they sell.

But the copy written on the packaging (and subsequently the website and e-newsletter) made it so much more. It conveyed 'goodness' in its naïve, 'innocent' tone, a little gentle humour, and the feeling that they took what they did seriously without taking themselves too seriously.

Lots of FMCG (fast moving consumer goods) brands have tried to ape their style ever since.

In the early days, I think most Innocent copy was written by one guy. So it was easy to have a consistent, distinctive tone of voice.

It's unlikely you'll be in that situation – you're normally writing for a brand that's already established.

Handy hint

To get a feel for the brand voice, try personification. Marlboro invented 'The Marlboro Man' to sell its cigarettes. It was a phenomenal success and one of the longest-running brand campaigns of all time. To write copy for Marlboro, you might simply imagine you were The Marlboro Man, since he is the personification of the brand. Then write with his voice.

'Become' whichever brand you're working on, and it will help you choose the right:

- ideas to express
- words to choose
- sentence construction
- tone to adopt.

For many years I wrote for a financial services brand that wanted a kind of Jamie Oliver personality.

Not saying 'pukka' or 'sweet as' every other sentence, but having his kind of exuberance and way of expressing ideas in a no-nonsense but matey way.

It's fantastic if a company can define their brand personality so clearly; many won't. In which case it's up to you to imagine what kind of person the brand would be like, by looking at the best of what they are and want to be.

When you know how they want to make their audience feel, you can work out what kind of person would make the audience feel that way.

Tourism Ireland was a client of mine, and it didn't have a particularly distinct personality. I felt that, when talking about a country famous for its Blarney, a friendly tone that had a slight Irish lilt might work well.

That didn't mean saying 'to be sure' or 'eejit' or 'top of the morning' in the copy. Just gentle Irishisms like sometimes saying 'yourself' instead of 'you' or 'so you will' or even just 'sláinte' (meaning cheers). Or Irish use of tenses, such as 'You'll be after me showing you around the place', or 'Go exploring once you have your breakfast eaten.'

I'd look up Irish sayings and proverbs, listen to audio of Irish people talking and make notes of the language the Irish clients used when I went to see them. The result was lilting, lyrical copy across web, press, mail and email that helped define the brand and began to get across the warm, informal experience of taking a break in Ireland… so it did.

Good books on brand I've read include *Eating the Big Fish* by Adam Morgan, considered something of a classic nowadays, as is *No logo* by Naomi Klein and *The Brand Gap* by Marty Neumeier.

And if you want a good example of how one writer can change their tone of voice to suit the context, try the novel *Cloud Atlas* by David Mitchell – a tour de force of different characters each with their own voice and idiolect.

Now, there's no reason why you can't write copy that is not only perfectly 'on brand', it actually helps crystallise what the brand is for everyone involved.

When David Abbott wrote those iconic *Economist* ads, from *'"I never read the Economist." Management trainee, aged 42'* onwards, he wasn't just creating great advertising.

He was helping his client get a better sense of what their own brand *could* and *should* be – an intelligent, thought-provoking and witty way to make you feel that 'You'll do better in business when you read the Economist'.

So: there's no excuse for writing the same way on different brands.

They spend a huge amount of time and money on their brand, so your words must sound like *their* words. If, when you personify the brand, you get copy where 'They just wouldn't put it like that', then don't use it. No matter how good you think it is.

Some brands are breathless and exclamatory (like Gala Bingo, another client I wrote for). Some are witty (like the Economist). Some like to put things as simply and succinctly as possible and generally avoid wit (like Dyson, another client I've written for. Instead, their voice was that of 'a passionate engineer').

Learn the brand and use the words, tone, construction, phraseology and punctuation that makes it sound like the brand is talking through you. Look at the best work that's been done for that brand so far. Copy some of the expressions, turns of phrase and meter.

Because (usually) lots of different copywriters will all work on the same brand, it's only by those writers supporting and reinforcing each other's copy that different communications will sound like they're coming from the same one voice.

---

ii. Audience

Allegedly, when Coca-Cola first entered China, it was translated as *Ke-kou-ke-la*. Which means 'Bite the wax tadpole'. Eventually they found a close phonetic equivalent, *Ko-kou-ko-le*, which means 'Happiness in the mouth'.

Pepsi's luck was no better. Their slogan 'Come Alive with the Pepsi Generation' became 'Pepsi brings your ancestors back from the grave'.

In Africa, where there's a large proportion of people who can't read, it's common to put a picture of a tin's contents on the label, so someone who's illiterate knows what's inside. Gerber didn't know that, so their baby food… had a picture of a baby on the side.

And when P&G launched Camay in Japan, they stuck to the same TV ad format they'd used in other countries, where men and women complimented each other on their appearance.

The ads failed because in Japan, culturally men and women simply didn't do that.

Which all goes to show: just as it's important to know who's talking (the brand), it's also important for the brand to know who it's talking to. What they'll easily understand. What's appropriate for them. And what will resonate with them.

We looked at this a bit in 1.4 of this book – how pen portraits can give you an idea of who you're talking to. As well as how it can help if you imagine you're talking to someone you know who fits the demographic of your target audience.

But there are finer nuances to think about, according to the audience's relationship with the the brand / product / service.

For example, are they a 'cold' audience (one that you don't have a relationship with)? Do they know the brand? Well, or only a bit? Are they likely to have a competitor product?

If Apple is talking to fanboys (as they'd get at one of their events), then their language might be a little different from in their advertising. Which might differ again according to whether it's in a market where a competitor might dominate, or one where Apple is the market leader. It might vary according to whether they're selling a more technical product, such as a piece of video editing software, compared to a more universal product, such as an iPhone.

The brand stays the same, the personality is unchanged. But the strength of that personality, the subtleties within it, might flex according to the audience.

So ask: What does the audience currently think and feel about your subject and brand? What do you *want* them to think / feel? Now: what's it going to take to move them from the former to the latter?

My favourite example of understanding the audience (and the brand) comes from clothing catalogue company Boden (whose founder, Johnny Boden, apparently writes much of the copy, with a famously idiosyncratic style).

The story I've heard is that one year they sent out their Mini Boden catalogue and it featured a kid's t-shirt with a picture of a toy revolver on it. They got a lot of complaints.

So allegedly, Mr Boden sent an email to their customers. Apologising at length for the t-shirt. Saying it was a mistake. Remarking that, "We feel stupid. Especially me."

And what do you know? Allegedly the next catalogue achieved record sales. The audience felt Boden understood them. Shared the same values. And most of all, listened to them.

In fact, I spoke to someone who used to work for Boden who said that after that, they considered whether or not they should find *more* reasons to apologise to their customers, since it seemed to be so good for sales.

Don't get too hung up on the audience though.

It's important to know who they are, what they're like and what relationship they have with the brand you're writing for. But as long as you keep that in mind, you're doing okay.

The brand will attract a certain type of audience – according to whether it's a brand designed to convey value, simplicity, coolness, exclusivity, superiority and so on. So as long as the brand is right and your copy is 'on brand', it should, in the broad brush, have the right tone for the general audience.

After that, you can concentrate on engaging and persuading them.

One final point on writing for an audience. Sometimes you'll be required to magically create a communication that's perfectly aimed at two (or more) distinct audiences.

Which is tricky.

Handy hint

The only practical answer is to write your copy to whatever aspects the audiences have in common, particularly tonally. If you put what you know about each audience in a Venn diagram, you're writing to the middle bit where they all overlap. Although, as you can imagine, writing to this more homogenous group isn't ideal, and can knock the edges off your copy.

Then, you can distinguish between them when talking about specifics, such as 'If you've recently become a parent... On the other hand, if your children are already at school...'.

---

iii. Medium

Great copy is great copy, whatever the medium.

But copy does work differently according to the environment in which it appears. Often for simple physical reasons – such as the amount of space afforded, or the way audiences consume those media, or the things you're able to do in one medium that you can't do in another.

At the stating-the-bleeding-obvious level, you've got less space in an online banner ad than you have in a mail pack. And someone taking the tube will spend less time seeing an escalator ad than a crosstrack (the ads across the tracks at tube stations).

At the not-so-bleeding-obvious level... well, it can take a whole career to learn the minutiae that are pertinent to an individual medium, but much of that will come down to four things:

1. The brands which use those media
2. The audiences that consume those media
3. The physical opportunities / constraints of those media (which, with a little bit of head-scratching, you can often work out)
4. The nature of how / when / why the audience consume those media.

We've already looked at brands and audiences, so let's look at 3. and 4. It won't give you a lifetime's worth of knowledge in a few sentences, but it should get you started if you're working in an unfamiliar medium – say if you normally write / review mail packs, but are occasionally called upon to write a quarter-page press ad or come up with a blog piece for the company website.

In the *Examples* section of this book are samples of copy I've written in different media. So you can see how I approach copy differently according the medium I'm writing for.

But here are a few pointers for seven media you might commonly work in:

1. Press

Double page spread, full page, half page, quarter page, 20 double, feature-link, advertorial…

…these are just some of the many types of press ad. And that's before you look at whether it's in full colour or not, what publication it's going to appear in and whether or not it's a special with a tip-on (something stuck onto the ad) or some other unusual feature.

Height (in centimetres) is first, width (by number of columns) is second. So '20 double' means an ad 20 centimetres high, two columns across. The columns are what the publication divides its pages into (creating a grid for its layouts, and columns of copy for its articles). Look at *The Times*, for instance – every page is divided into five columns of type.

A feature-link ad in regional press means you supply info for a journalist to write an article (on a topic that's relevant to your ad), and in a moment of great serendipity, your ad appears right alongside the feature.

An advertorial is an advert designed to look like an article in the paper, usually given away by having ADVERTISEMENT FEATURE written across the top.

What you do in the space you have depends entirely on your brand, audience, subject and your imagination. If you've an image, a headline and maybe even a reply coupon, but only a half page ad, then there's not going to be much room for more than 20 or 30 words.

On the other hand, there have been some fantastic full page ads that have been 800 words long. Some longer than that. It's worth remembering that if someone's reading a newspaper or magazine, then they're comfortable reading long copy – since that's what a newspaper or magazine consists of. In fact, they bought the publication because they *like* reading long copy.

So as long as your long copy is utterly captivating for that audience, there's no reason to imagine that tall towers of words will put them off.

If you're doing a classic headline + image press ad, hold dear to the 'one straight, one twisted' maxim. So don't make both headline and image utterly straightforward, or you'll have a dull ad. And don't make both the image and the line clever, or you'll have a confusing ad.

Instead, if you have a clever headline, persuade the art director to have a straightforward, clear image. Or if you're using a 'witty' image, have a straight, clear headline.

One of the classic VW Beetle ads had the headline 'Lemon'. That intriguing headline is the 'twisted' part, so the image is 'straight'; simply a picture of the Beetle.

Conversely, a great, award-winning ad for a VW Polo many years later has a witty image instead. It's a wedding photograph where the bride and groom are out of focus, because the photographer has focussed on the bus in the distance behind them, which has the line 'Polo L £8,240' written on the side.

It's a clever concept – the idea that the price is so astonishing, the photographer is focusing on that rather than the bride and groom. So this time, because it's the image that's 'twisted', the line is straight: it simply says Surprisingly ordinary prices.

You don't have to have an image and headline to make it a good press ad of course. One of my favourite series of press ads were for Tesco. One of those, for instance, just had a picture of an apple with no headline. The copy read: 'Granny Smiths. What's the difference between ours and our competitor's? Not much really. They're the same quality as Waitrose. And the same price as Asda.'

2. TV

TV advertising is still one of the media that copywriters most desire to work in. Big budget campaigns, anyway. Not so much those cheap daytime 'Have you been involved in an accident at work?' ads.

TV ads can be sliced up in a number of ways, including awareness TV, BRTV, DRTV, high budget and low budget. One offs and long-running campaigns. There are 10", 30", 60" and 90" long ads, three minute 'infomercials', there are bumper ads (those where a brand is sponsoring a programme) and more.

Plus there's always the joy of getting your ad approved by *Clearcast* – no other medium requires you to get your work approved by an independent body before it can run. Unless you're doing a TV ad as a viral which will only appear online, in which case you can tell *Clearcast* to clear off.

If you want to feel envious, read *Get Smashed* by Sam Delaney – an account of advertising life in the 1980s. Back then, clients poured money into big budget TV commercials without any mention of ROI (return on investment). Nowadays, clients do a great deal of research and audience focus group testing before putting 'significant spend' into a commercial.

There's a Barnardo's ad I really like that makes its budget go further very cleverly. The first half of the ad tells the 'before' part of the story, the second half tells the 'after'. But the first half comprises clips 1, 2, 3, 4 while the voiceover (the girl in the ad) explains how she got into trouble, and the second half shows the same clips (in reverse order 4, 3, 2, 1) while the girl explains how she got out of trouble, thanks to Barnardo's. So in the second half it's the same bits of film, but they mean something different.

A copywriter's role in a TV ad is in helping originate and shape the idea. After that you may have a voiceover, you may have dialogue in the ad, there may be 'supers' (words that appear over the image on screen), there even be some copy that's seen in the ad. Or there may be none of that; it might just be a great piece of film with a rousing soundtrack.

Which doesn't matter: don't feel that copywriting means you need to force words in there – coming up with a great idea and nurturing it throughout the process is the biggest contribution you can make.

There are three related things I can tell you from my experience of making TV ads that I'd like to share:

- Firstly, think about how your idea can be expressed as simply as possible. Because the process of making the ad will tend to make every element more complex.
- Secondly, expect about twenty times as many people to be involved in the making of 'your' TV ad as in any other medium you've worked in.

- Thirdly, chaperone, protect and champion your ad all the way from your first storyboard to the time it first airs on TV.

The first point is that because TV is a very technical medium, involving filming, sound recording, music, actors, special effects and so on, it's easy for every element to a) become more complicated along the way and b) get interpreted along the way, so they end up not fitting together as well as they did in your head. Keeping the idea as clear and simple as possible really helps. In the *Examples* section of this book you'll find a really simple TV ad I did.

Secondly, it really is remarkable how many people it takes to make even a basic ad.

For a start, the client will suddenly appear at the shoot. Bet they've never expressed an interest in watching a banner ad get made, have they? Then there are the number of people involved in casting, rehearsing, shooting, editing, post-production. Every ad feels like you're remaking Ben Hur. Except instead of a cast of thousands, it's a crew of thousands.

And thirdly, because of the previous two points, it's really important that you keep sight of what it is you're trying to achieve and that you let everyone involved know. Everyone should have a common understanding of what they're working towards.

The most important two people to work with are the producer and the director.

Make sure you and they all agree on the nature of the ad, what it's trying to do and what feel you want to capture. I've worked on ads before where the director has had their own agenda and hasn't cared one fig about making the ad we briefed, or something that would work well for the client. The result was a self-indulgent mess and it was my fault for not standing up to the director during the shoot.

Right at the start, when you're working on the idea, have a feel for the budget. Every time you add an actor or a location, you're adding cost. Having dialogue in the ad rather than a voiceover takes longer to shoot, so costs more. Buying existing music can be cheaper or more expensive than originating the music, depending on what you're after.

Handy hint

Shooting in an outdoor location is more expensive than shooting in a studio. Shooting a scene in Leicester Square is going to be much more expensive than shooting on a hill in Scotland. Bear all this in mind because it's usually better to have a well executed, more polished ad set in three locations than a hurried, cut-corners ad set in five.

Also be very aware of the length of the ad. If you have a voiceover, read it out loud and time it again and again. A hurried voiceover in the final edit does your ad no favours at all.

And lastly, don't be discouraged.

Apparently, the Guinness 'surfer' ad (find it online if you don't know it) tested really badly with focus groups. They absolutely hated it. But the client was brave enough to trust the creative team and get it made anyway (not cheaply, since it was shot in Hawaii).

It went on to win shedloads of awards, be massively popular with the audience, see a resurgence in Guinness sales, and be voted the greatest ad of all time by the public in 2001. And the voiceover? Excerpts from *Moby Dick*. Now there's powerful copy for you.

3. Mail

Direct mail has a number of things going for it for a copywriter:

- you have a number of elements, so you can tell the story in layers, and give different roles to different items within the pack
- you usually have a letter, often around 700 words, giving you a 'long copy' opportunity to persuade the audience
- because you're writing to a named individual, you're likely to have some useful insights about them, so your copy can be more tailored.

An agency I was at tried writing 'male' and 'female' copy versions for a client. The male version was more to-the-point, more focussed on factual detail, using bullet points to list things. The female copy was more storytelling and more emotive, less focussed on the nitty gritty.

The male copy did better to men than the female copy to men; the female copy did better to women than the male copy to women. And the difference was statistically significant.

The fourth great joy of direct mail is that there's a lot you can do with the medium. With a 48 sheet billboard, then yes you can use light sensitive ink, or superglue a car to the side of it, or change it every day for a week. But generally, you've got the same landscape rectangle which you can print on.

With direct mail, there are a million different things you can do.

I've done packs that have used 'seed paper' which you can plant afterwards and watch grow into flowers. Packs with holes all the way through them. Packs impregnated with the smell of cut grass. Packs containing sweets or a sachet of aftersun cream or a piece of string or a cartridge of red ink to represent blood. Packs where something flew out when you opened it.

I've done mailings that played audio when you opened them (see the *Examples* section). Ones with all sorts of different die-cut shapes or bits of embossing or scratch-off areas or unusual stock (paper). Big packs, little packs, thin packs, fat packs. Digitally printed packs (where you can personalise every image, if you want). A one-piece mailer stuck to a piece of astro turf.

In a mail pack there's almost always something more interesting you can do with a piece of paper than make it a leaflet. Make 'What can we do that's more interesting than a leaflet?' your starting point.

Spend time on how you can use the medium in a way that's interesting, but relevant to your message.

The fifth great advantage of direct mail is that everything you do is measurable. You can run one idea against another and see which gets the most response. You can test a shocking idea against a comforting one. Long copy against short copy. One offer against another.

Think of the outer envelope as a press ad space. If you do a 'reverse flap' outer (one where the window for the address to show through and the envelope's flap are both on the same side) then on the other side you've got a useful space, whether portrait or landscape, to create intrigue or provocation or make a promise.

Handy hint

One thing to ensure with direct mail is that your concept tracks through the whole pack.

I've seen too many packs where the concept is entirely on the outer; you open it and it's just by-the-numbers junk mail with scant regard for the concept it began with. Think about how every element can contribute to the concept, which stems from the proposition. Combined with a well-written, personal letter, it can make for a very effective medium.

Handy hint

Just as you may have a hierarchy of information, have a hierarchy of size in the mailing too. Put the most important stuff on the biggest element (usually the letter). Put the least important information on the smallest element in the pack.

Doordrops, by the way, are often treated the same way as direct mail, just without the person's name and address on.

To understand the fundamentals of the medium, I'd recommend Commonsense Direct Marketing by Drayton Bird.

4. *Inserts*

Inserts are those things that fall out of your newspaper / magazine. Which everyone finds irritating. And inserts are what you might call a 'low interest medium'. They get very poor response rates, but they're produced in high volumes at a low unit cost to make it worthwhile.

There are a few things worth knowing about copywriting for inserts – in addition to the obvious point that since they're so low interest, you need to work extra hard to grab attention.

Firstly, if someone's reading a newspaper or magazine… they like reading. So, as with press ads, write something interesting, and who knows, they might just read it.

Secondly, when clients get falling results from inserts, they tend to cut back to smaller and smaller formats. But actually, there's evidence that by 'building cost in' and creating larger, longer inserts with more (well written) copy, you'll get a better response which more than compensates for the extra production cost.

Especially as, unlike in other media, a newspaper or magazine doesn't charge more for a bigger or heavier insert (up to its size limits).

If you know the publication the insert is going in, tailor the copy to suit. Usually the newspaper or magazine is chosen because it's what the target audience reads anyway, but if it's going in Home & Gardens, for instance, then read the magazine, get a feel for their style and content and what interests their readers, and write the insert in a similar way, almost as if it were a magazine supplement.

5. Digital

It's laughably vague to summarise all online media as 'digital'. You might be writing copy for websites, emails, apps, blogs, tweets, SEO, banner ads, drop-down ads, adwords…

…in fact, it's pretty vague to just refer to 'websites' when there are dozens of broad categories of website.

But digital media can be usefully divided into three types. *Bought, earned* and *owned.*

Bought means anything you pay for – like ads on other people's websites or searches or sponsored links. Earned means anything that doesn't cost you media space – social media when people are talking about you on Facebook or Twitter or in the comments section of the BBC website, for example. Owned, unsurprisingly, means media you already own – like your own website.

Each type has its own strengths, but one thing that's very useful is to encourage them to interact. Write a blog on your owned media that you can link to (and get talked about) in earned media, for instance.

Social media may be where the action is (as well as the most difficult to get right). But infuriatingly, it's also the area that can be least directly affected by copywriting. Since, by its 'social' nature, it's more about what everyone else is writing, not you.

The other thing, of course, is that the 'digital space' changes at a rapid pace. Giants of social media come and go (remember *Friends Reunited? Bebo?*). New ways to reach your audience appear like bright, colourful butterflies… with just as short a lifespan.

There are lots of good resources online about writing online. As well as plenty of guides to the different sub-categories within 'online' and what all the terms mean. There's also a 'case study' for an email and a blog in the *Examples* section.

To avoid this book covering topics that will continue to change, here are five generalisations I've acquired during my time of 'doing digital':

i. 'The digital space' has quickly become one of the most interactive, involving and (in a virtual way) 'social' mediums of all. People are comfortable with providing a lot more personal information about themselves than they ever have in any other medium at any time in history. As a consequence, they expect you to know who they are and tailor your content accordingly.

ii. Technical innovation sometimes outpaces need. Sometimes it gives you options for fancy-pants effects that don't really add to your work. Be wary not to do things just because you can, rather than because it helps your copy.

iii. Write briefly. Shorter words. Shorter sentences. Shorter paragraphs. Snippier snippets. What doesn't look like much copy on a page looks a lot longer online, an area where people are click-happy and have very short attention spans. Ernest Hemingway would have been a good online writer; sparse, meaty copy.

iv. Don't ignore the technical considerations: consult a cyber-geek (they are, in my experience, always very willing to share their knowledge). For example, search engine optimisation (SEO) is a whole discipline in its own right, which you may not be interested in learning.

So instead, check with someone who knows that for SEO, the key words should be in the headline. That the nearer the front of the headline, the better. And that the title might be best under 72 characters, so it appears in full in search results.

Or someone who knows that many emails are viewed – and actioned – just in the preview pane. And that around 50% of people never scroll an email. Giving you another reason to get to the point very quickly in email comms.

v. Ask people to get involved, and they often will (partly, perhaps, because digital media make it so easy to). Say 'Please retweet' and you'll get many times more retweets than if you rely on just being relevant and interesting and *hoping* people will retweet. Asking people on Facebook to get involved in a flashmob or some other event can reap dividends. Ask people to link, ask people to comment, ask people for their ideas and opinions.

All of this interactivity is an important part of what online is about, so make it an integral part of your copy – don't just stick a cut-down quarter-page press ad into a banner ad, or turn a direct mail letter into a passive email.

Greenpeace asked people to forward an email message to Nestlé, asking them to stop using palm oil sourced from environmentally-unfriendly suppliers. It worked. Then they asked people to forward a message to HSBC, asking them to stop funding those same suppliers. That worked too.

Getting it wrong. The moderator of the Nestlé Facebook page got it wrong big time. When people altered the Nestlé logo as their avatar on the fan page, the administrator told them their messages would be deleted, along with sarcastic, condescending comments and a lofty 'We make the rules' mantra. It spiralled horribly, with a tremendous backlash against Nestlé's Big Brother approach. A PR nightmare, they eventually had to apologise… and allow a lot of negative commentary and threats of boycotting to build up. All as a result of their misunderstanding of 'The power of the crowd' that exists online.

See also 'Gillian McKeith / Ben Goldacre / Twitter' for another example of getting it wrong, in this case when McKeith (allegedly) seemed to badly misunderstand the medium she was using.

The last thing I'd say about digital is that in its non-social forms (emails, web pages, ads) it's even better than direct mail at enabling you to test different offers and executions very quickly and easily.

For instance, smart banner ads that show products you've previously looked at on the advertiser's website. Or web pages that use your computer's IP address to bring in information relevant to your location.

6. Radio

I've really enjoyed the radio I've been involved with. In some ways, it's a very 'pure' form of copywriting: apart from a few (usually cheesy) sound effects, a radio ad is just your copy read or performed aloud. Pure and unadulterated.

Many radio ads are awful, of course: they overreach massively and are delivered very hammily. But they needn't be. You can create a picture in the mind very easily with radio. You're unlikely to come up against budget constraints, and the sound of someone talking to you, albeit in an ad, can feel very intimate and personal. Just think of ideas that get the reader to imagine the scene, to paint their own picture.

Don't treat it as a TV script that needs more sound effects to compensate for the fact that people can't see it.

Handy hint

Just as important as in TV is being sure of the script length. Edit ruthlessly so that your ad has enough 'air' and so the voiceover artist can give the right inflection and emphasis to the script, rather than having to take a deep breath and hurtle through it.

7. Poster

Your classic 48 sheet poster has a headline of eight words… at most.

Handy hint

Make sure you work with the art director to establish the best typographical layout for your copy. Since your whole copy is probably no more than eight words, make sure they have a layout that supports them – and try as many different iterations of the line as possible: try changing different words, changing the order of the words, cutting down the number of words.

The first expression of the line you come up with may be the best one, but you can't be sure until you've tried 50 others.

I saw a billboard the other day that read: 'You can tell it's been made by people who care about cider'. 12 words. What was wrong with 'Cider made by people who care'? It's half as many words and it makes the product category the first word, rather than the last. Still a boring line though.

Some of the best posters have no words. Which doesn't mean the copywriter wasn't involved in coming up with the idea, just that they were secure enough in their wordsmithery to embrace an idea that didn't need words. Honest.

Billboards are big spaces that need work of big impact. And you get big impact by having a single-minded idea expressed with as few elements as possible. Less really is more in posters. Look at it this way: the more elements you have, the less attention each individual element can get.

If someone's driving past your poster, they may only have time to take in one element. Which you've just reduced the impact of by adding a strapline as well as a headline. Or by writing eight words when it could have been done in two.

Like the Burger King ad for fiery fries: the line was just 'Fiery fries' next to a giant chip, the end dipped in ketchup to make it look like a match. Or the famous Wonderbra ad 'Hello Boys' with a traffic-stopping image of Eva Herzigova looking down at her own cleavage.

One of my favourites had no image, and the headline (which took up the entire space) was 13 words long, breaking the first rule of billboard copy. It was for the RSPCA and read 'A battery hen lives in a space the size of this full stop.' The full stop was about the size of a folded newspaper – the size of a battery hen's cage.

Posters are a very 'immediate' medium. Don't try and be too clever and don't try and tell too much of the story. A single thought is absolutely critical for a poster. Which may be why so many posters are so bland: rather than agreeing on a single, sharp thing to say, the team involved had to settle on saying nothing at all. Vaguely.

Handy hint

So there you are. A whistle-stop tour of some of the media you might work in. *Hey Whipple, Squeeze This* by Luke Sullivan is a great book about advertising and different media, with examples of work for different brands, audiences and media. Also try *Cutting Edge Advertising* by Jim Aitchison (specifically for print media).

But if you're working in a medium you're unfamiliar with, talk to someone who does know it. Don't be afraid to ask them what the jargon they'll inevitably slip into means.

And as an overarching rule, remember that every medium has its own strengths, weaknesses and nuances. Simply copying and pasting your work from one medium to another is not going to do your copy justice.

Now for some hocus pocus.

All that *Content* and *Context* prep has gathered together your eye of newt, phlegm of bat, dried mandrake root and the sigh from a melancholic mermaid.

Now we blend them together in our copy cauldron. But to create something truly magical, we need a concept and a style to bring the ingredients to life and a structure to hold it all together.

Sometimes you'll do these three sub-steps – *concept, style* and *structure* – before you start your first draft. Sometimes you just have a rough feel for them and they emerge more clearly as you write. Either way, somewhere during *Create* is where you write your first draft.

And to help with your hubble, bubble, toil and trouble, I commend two very useful allies to you: SOPHIE and BOB.

Concept,
style &
structure

---

i. Concept

Just before we bring in SOPHIE, let me make the obvious point that not all copy needs a concept.

If you're writing an email to a friend, for instance, you'd be unlikely to give it a concept. Unless you were the sort of person whose dinner also came with a concept.

But, if you're writing copy for business communications, coming up with concepts is probably going to be an important part of your job.

What do we mean by a concept? Well, I mean a creative idea that doesn't yet exist in the subject, the proposition, the brand or anything else. It's a new idea that invigorates your communication or campaign and gives it an identity of its own.

Okay. SOPHIE is an acronym to sense-check any concept you come up with.

It stands for *Simple, Original, Powerful, Honed, Intelligent* and *Emotive.*

They're all pretty self-explanatory and we've gone over them in other parts of this book. But here, we're judging the concept against these values, which we can pair up into three couplets.

1. Your concept should be Simple & Original.

This is the toughest couplet of all: coming up with an idea that's both simple and original.

Coming up with a simple idea is relatively easy. Trouble is, lots of the best simple ideas have already been done. The simple way to express the emotional benefit of insurance, for instance, is *peace of mind.* As a result, that hoary old phrase has been used in three quarters of the insurance communications out there for decades.

Coming up with an original idea is also relatively easy, if you just go mental. Chances are no-one's ever made sprout, toothpaste and wine gum casserole before. It would be original. But probably not very good.

No, finding an idea that's both simple *and* original (or at the very least, *fresh,* if original is too lofty an ambition) requires you to sit quietly and scratch your brain with a sharpened pencil.

And if you're brave enough, show people the idea. Do they get it straight away? Or do you have to keep explaining it to them, before they eventually say, "Oh… I see" (in which case it's not simple enough). Or do they say, "Oh, I loved it when Sony did that" (in which case it's not original enough).

For example

The tagline for a new Audi sports car: Mirror, Signal, Outmaneuver. Three words. Only three letters of which are different from a well-known driving phrase. Really simple. Yet I've never seen it used as the lead concept for a car before.

2. Your concept should be Powerful & Honed.

Powerful and honed just mean making every aspect of the concept *even more so.*

Go back to the first two: simple and original. How could you make your idea simpler? What could you lose from it to make the idea clearer, more immediate? How could you make it more original? What twist or frisson of newness could you add to lift it above the 'seen it before' category? How could you amplify the idea, turn up the volume and make it more attention-grabbing, more engaging, more persuasive?

This is not a time for lily-livered whisperers, humbly suggesting their wares. This is a time for potent, irresistible voices, for mighty orators who have vast audiences hanging on their every word. Make your concept as potent as it can possibly be.

3. Your concept should be Intelligent & Emotive.

We've looked at this symbiotic relationship before. The yin and yang of your *writing,* the concept should appeal to both hearts and minds too.

So be wary of concepts that are cold, intellectual exercises lacking in emotion (although sometimes the emotion in a concept can be the warm feeling people get from understanding your clever reference).

Consider your concept from both angles and if it's lacking a rational or emotional aspect, work out how to add whichever is absent frome the idea. Just consider what missing *thought* or *feeling* you could bring in to your concept.

The Nike award-winning 'Write the future' TV ad had a simple, original concept with an idea that appealed to people's minds: inventively imagining what famous footballers' future lives might be like after doing well at the World Cup. But the concept was also rich with emotion, with moving music, slo-mo action and cheering crowds that stirred the blood and made you want to be part of it (by buying Nike, obviously).

For example

So that's SOPHIE. Remember her three couplets and you'll know what to look for in your concepts.

Now; how to come up with them. Enter stage right: BOB.

"Oh, for a muse of fire that would ascend the brightest heaven of invention!" begins Shakespeare's Henry V.

Sometimes, with a deadline pressing and an uninspiring brief, a muse of any kind can be hard to come by.

That's why over the years I've gathered, developed and post-rationalised lots of ways of developing concepts. Together, they make up BOB – the Book Of Brainwaves. Using it helps prevent you from getting into a rut of coming up with the same sort of ideas over and over again.

There are 20 techniques in the Book of Brainwaves – if you come up with more, please let me know.

Of course, you probably won't get a chance to try all 20 techniques on every job. Perhaps just half a dozen. So I'd recommend spending time becoming comfortable with all 20 and then on every project use the same three or four approaches that seem to work best for you, plus another couple from the list, changing which two on every brief.

Then, spend 30-60 minutes coming up with as many ideas as you can using the first technique on your list. Then 30-60 minutes with the next technique, and so on.

Once you have a big raft of ideas, stick them all on the wall, stand back and see which ones stand out. Use BAM and SOPHIE to sense check them.

Then take the most promising two or three ideas and spend a few more hours with SOPHIE to push each one on.

Before you start using the techniques in BOB, spend half an hour or so capturing your 'top of head' ideas – the stuff that's already occurred to you as you've gone through the brief and researched the subject.

You might find that many of them are 'the usual suspects' – they came to you unbidden because they're the obvious ideas which are most likely to have been done many times before. But it's good to capture them, even if just to cleanse the mental palate.

Plus, any of them might help inspire a bolder, fresher idea when you start going through your BOB techniques.

The Book of Brainwaves:

1. Dramatise	11. Think random link
2. Factualise	12. Topical
3. Reframe	13. Analogy
4. Image led	14. Invention
5. Copy led	15. Perspective-shift
6. Typographic	16. Pastiche / parody
7. Provoke	17. Sensual
8. Compare	18. Play with the medium / format
9. Storytelling	19. Become another
10. Challenge convention	20. Combine and refine

1. Dramatise

Exaggerate and dramatise the proposition until it becomes
creatively compelling.

Since the proposition is usually around the key benefit,
promise or solution to a problem, dramatising that benefit will
nearly always give you a strong concept. So this approach
is always at the top of my list.

*An idea we came up with for Husqvarna, who make those sit-on
lawnmowers for rich people with big gardens. One of the key benefits
was that large lawns could be mowed quickly and easily. To dramatise
that to an extreme: what if it made mowing your lawn so quick, it was
as if your lawn felt tiny to mow? So we designed a one-piece mailing
stuck to an A5-sized piece of astro turf, with the line 'Makes mowing
so easy, it's as if your lawn's this big.'*

For
example

Alternatively, instead of dramatising the key product / service / offer / benefit you'll find in the proposition, you could dramatise one of the 32 universal 'What's In It For Me' motivations from 1.4 of this book. To recap, they are:

1. to be liked	17. to be happy
2. to be loved	18. to have fun
3. to be popular	19. to gain knowledge
4. to be appreciated / valued	20. to be healthy
5. to be right	21. to satisfy curiosity
6. to feel important	22. for convenience
7. to make money	23. out of fear
8. to save money	24. out of greed
9. to save time	25. out of guilt
10. to make work easier	26. to belong
11. to be secure	27. to gain respect
12. to be attractive	28. to avoid pain
13. to be sexy	29. to get pleasure
14. to be comfortable	30. to give life meaning
15. to stand out	31. to achieve something
16. to fit in	32. to win

Back to Husqvarna, we could have developed ideas around 17, 'to be happy' and talked about how mowing your lawn with a Husqvarna was one of Sunday morning's great pleasures. Along with reading the papers, having a lazy breakfast… and having a lie-in, which you were able to do thanks to how quick a Husqvarna made mowing the lawn (so from a WIIFM emotional benefit back to a product rational benefit).

You can also dramatise the problem you're offering to solve, of course. Like the ad for a haemorrhoid cream that showed toilet roll made from sandpaper, dramatising the 'discomfort' of having piles.

2. Factualise

Find a fact or figure or stat and use that. A surprising fact can be very effective, because it can be creatively engaging and utterly truthful. The stat may be directly connected with your subject, or related to it more indirectly, if it helps illustrate your message.

The poster for Cancer Research UK that shows three little girls sat with their backs to us, looking out over some fields. There's one word above each of them: 'Lawyer, Teacher, Cancer', highlighting the fact that one in three people will be affected by cancer.

Or the WWF mailing – the letter headline says 'This letter contains 300 words – one for every snow leopard left in Nepal.'

The other way you can use this technique is to discover a fact (rather than a stat) about your subject and then lead with that.

The classic Rolls Royce print ad from yesteryear, where the headline read 'At 60 miles an hour, the loudest noise in this new Rolls Royce comes from the ticking of its electric clock'.

3. Reframe

Just as you might rewrite a headline a dozen different ways, try doing the same with the proposition.

Change the words, write it so it says basically the same thing but in another way. Imagine how different people might express the same thought… just find as many ways as you can to rephrase and reframe the proposition. It'll often give you a new way to look at the core message that could form the basis of a new concept.

The proposition for British Airways was 'The world's biggest airline'. But it's clear how much more interesting your concepts and copy can be when you simply rephrase it as 'The world's favourite airline'.

4. Image led

Shock horror: just because you're a copywriter doesn't mean all your ideas have to be word-based.

Think of photography, illustrations or optical illusions that could lead the idea. Either with no headline or just a straightforward one.

For example

When Harvey Nichols opened their Bristol store, they showed Wallace and Gromit (developed by Aardman Animations who are based in Bristol) dressed in designer gear.

You can also use imagery to be less literal and just convey a feeling.

For example

A Waitrose ad for lamb that showed a close-up of a shepherd's hands on his crook with fields in the background, with a simple line saying the type of lamb and the price. It got across a feeling of 'good provenance' and didn't show the product at all, or try to be clever with a highbrow concept. Just gently conveyed a reassuring feeling of care and quality.

5. Copy led

Find an interesting way to describe the subject – with wit or a clever play on words or an attention-grabbing headline – and the whole idea can build from there.

Witty wordplay can engage an audience's mind, make them smile, feel clever… and become involved. There's a list of 20 ways to wax lyrical in the *Quick Tips* section of this book, from antithesis to puns to rhymes.

For example

The poster for Durex that simply said 'durex.org'.

A word of warning: there are some very bad pun ideas out there. For instance, a picture of Scottish moorland, with the headline 'Home insurance that's a breath of fresh air'.

You may laugh: I've seen plenty of work like that. Where the concept relies on artificially adding words to the line. Such as inserting 'refreshing' into the headline so you can show a picture of a cup of tea. The cup of tea has got nothing to do with the brand, the product or the proposition – and you've contrived to use it by using 'refreshing'.

I've also seen press ads for loans that say 'Hammering down the cost' and show a picture of a hammer.

That's very bad work. Don't do it.

6. Typographic

A concept around how you make the words appear. Use the font, layout, shape of the objects to form words, or look at how words are shown in other settings.

There's soooooooooo much we can do with type (like that, for instance).

Squash it in to a space while talking about something small or constrained. Expand it to convey relaxation. Make the words out of tools when talking about DIY. Use unusual fonts to create a certain feel. Distress the type. Make it look like a ransom note. Or a wanted ad. Or a crossword. Or a receipt. Or use punctuation or other symbols to convey an idea.

A mailing advertising Listerine Advanced Tartar Control sent to dental practices. The letter, talking about keeping your teeth white, was simply embossed words, so there was no print at all. Just raised white letters on a white background. Very clever. Hard to read, mind.

For example

7. Provoke

What's the most shocking, heart-rending, gut-wrenching, head-turning thing you can say?

Look at the subject and find a way to say something about it that will startle the audience. And look at what's *always* shocking too: swearing, violence, depravity, bad taste, cruelty, gore, political incorrectness, sex – and think about how that could relate to the work. Think of an idea that's immoral or illegal – you can then always tone it down so it becomes just about acceptable.

Why not try and provoke the audience by suggesting that they're lazy, stupid, ugly, wrong (about a fact, assumption, point of view) and then explaining why, or subverting their expectations – so it turns out we're not really insulting them.

For Dyson maybe we could show a dust mite up really close, so it looks like a disgusting, frightening creature, and tell the audience how many millions of them are breeding in your chair right now – unless you're using a Dyson.

Or for a children's charity, a headline saying 'I hate you, you worthless piece of shit' and then the copy could explain that that's what a child called Billy heard, over and over again, from his own mum.

8. Compare

Simply compare your subject with something else – show why your subject shares the same quality as something else good, or why it's different from something bad.

The most common comparison you'll see is the classic 'before and after'. Life before the product (terrible) compared to life after the product (wonderful).

The famous 'We washed half her hair in an ordinary shampoo, and half with new Head and Shoulders…' A simple, convincing demonstration of the product benefit.

There are many other ways to create comparisons (as well as an explanation of why it's so powerful) in the next section of this book, *Compel*.

9. Storytelling

Choose a storytelling genre and see how you could bring your subject to life with that theme.

Most people enjoy stories (and most people grow up with them from a very early age) so presenting the idea as some kind of story or situation can be very engaging.

Genres you might consider include:

- horror
- thriller
- adventure
- slapstick
- comedy
- action
- fairytale / fable
- love story
- period drama
- soap opera
- documentary
- news
- chat show
- reality show

Alternatively, think about how you might tell a story differently according to whether it was the story in a film, play, musical, graphic novel or book. There's a mailing that uses the storytelling concept in the *Examples* section.

10. Challenge convention

Ask yourself 'What if we *couldn't* do it that way? How else could it be done?'

Challenging the convention is good for coming up with bold ideas – and the bigger the convention you challenge, the bigger the idea you'll get.

It's useful because we make a lot of assumptions in almost everything we do. Usually those assumptions are handy shortcuts for getting things done, but they can mean we end up doing the same things in the same way, again and again – which isn't very creative.

Put the conventions / assumptions you've been working with under the microscope and ask *why* – why does it have to be done that way?

For example

If you're creating a mail pack, does it have to have a letter? Does it have to read top to bottom? Does it have to be about the subject? Does it have to be written by such-and-such, or could someone completely different sign it? Does it have to be in English?

An effective alternative to asking 'why' is to create an artificial problem to get around.

So you might say, 'Headlines must only be one word long' or 'The ad has to look like a six year old did it' or 'We're not allowed to mention the product name'.

Necessity is the mother of invention – so create a false necessity to come up with an inventive new approach.

For example

The iPhone is full of ideas which challenged conventions of the time. As a starter, the keyboard. Posing it as a problem, they could have said, 'How do we make a phone… when we're not allowed buttons?'

This could have led to the touch screen – one of the benefits being that when the keys aren't being used there's more area of the phone's 'real estate' given over to the screen. Another being that since the buttons are virtual, it's easy to customise and rearrange them.

11. Think random link

This is a lateral thinking exercise (developed by Edward de Bono) where you choose a random 'thing' and find a way to link it to the product / service / issue you're working with.

It forces our brain make a connection between the subject of the brief and something 'new' not normally associated with it. It doesn't always work, but when it does, it can lead to some very novel, off-the-wall ideas.

First, you need a simple thing. It can be a picture, an object (for example, flick through the Argos catalogue and choose a page and then item at random) or a simple noun.

Use a dictionary or a thesaurus or the list below (find a properly random way to select one), or use one of the many random word generators online.

84 random simple things:

elephant	secret	teabag	dictionary	plaster	chewing gum	bed
door	hair	wine	gym	lift	jeans	wheel
hurricane	ice-cream	watch	rocket	bath	banana	party
chair	flower	hospital	suitcase	snail	shoe	cinnamon
duvet	river	knife	butler	lunch	root	frog
jazz	smoke	dog	cloak	giraffe	hat	castle
button	periscope	drum kit	spear	taxi	litter	flamingo
book	shark	hat	lemon	leaf	verruca sock	starfish
prison	green	mouth	tracksuit	whisky	dustbin	oyster
rubber duck	peanut butter	beard	jelly	badge	mirror	vomit
crisp	chisel	budgie	flume	jumble sale	chip shop	firework

Once you have the 'thing', list three or four associations, functions or experiences from them. For instance, if the word was 'banana' you might write:

banana / yellow / food / bendy

You could then find a way to associate each of them in turn with the subject.

Persevere till your brain finds a link (the more you use this approach, the better you'll get at it). Sometimes random linking thinking will just give you the beginning of an idea – which you can then develop to make it more plausible.

For example

Here's an idea by lateral thinking's creator, Dr de Bono. His suggestion to help solve the conflict and unrest in the Middle East? Marmite.

His reasoning? They eat unleavened bread in the Middle East. No yeast. Which means they're missing out on zinc. And a zinc deficiency makes men irritable and belligerent. A few jars of zinc-rich marmite and everyone might be a lot nicer to each other.

12. Topical

Christmas, New Year, Valentine's Day, Spring, the anniversary of the subject, on this day in history – all ways of being topical that can drive a concept.

But also look at what's in the news and what the current zeitgeist is. What's likely to be going on in the lives of our audience? What stories are grabbing their attention?

You can also artificially create topicality, by creating some kind of event around your subject, whether physical or not.

For example

On the day George 'Dubya' Bush left the White House, under an article about his departure, Veet (hair removal cream for women) ran a small press ad: 'Goodbye Bush'.

Or a one-piece mailing I did for Avis, sent out when someone hired a car abroad so it would be on their doormat when they got back from their holiday in the sun – offering them a repeat booking discount. The mailing contained a real sachet of aftersun cream.

13. Analogy

Metaphors, similes and analogies can be great for copy – and for concepts too.

Look for something that is, in some way, like your subject (like the proposition of your subject).

For example

Volvo want to get across that their cars are safe, so they show a safety pin bent into a car shape.

Do sense-check them with other people though – it's easy to come up with an analogy that you think is great, but which other people just don't get. Analogies are a form of 'borrowed interest'. In the *Volvo* example above, for instance, it's borrowing the reputation a safety pin has for being safe. Which is fine; just be sure that what you're borrowing is obvious to your audience.

And generally, it's better to find something in your subject that's interesting, rather than having to borrow interest from elsewhere.

14. Invention

A really useful way to bring an issue, idea, problem or benefit to life is to create something that doesn't already exist.

Invent a person, a character, a term, a human condition, an alternative world, or even a word. All of these have been done very successfully for big campaigns.

One mentioned earlier, Marlboro Man – a character invented to personify what kind of person you'd be likened to if you smoked Marlboros. Perfect when you can't show or say much about cigarettes.

Or almost every shampoo commercial – they invent new pseudo-scientific words every time; 'Now enriched with Nutrilux, Shinieform and Glossimax'.

15. Perspective-shift

Take a different point of view. You could look at the subject through the eyes of someone unexpected, or change the time, to look at it from the past or the future.

Looking at it from someone else's point of view, there were some very moving 'stop smoking' TV ads. The smoker (who the ads were aimed at) wasn't featured in the ad at all. Instead, they were simply heart-breaking interviews with family members who'd lost someone to smoking-related cancer.

16. Pastiche / parody

Take something the audience will recognise and do a pastiche of it (or a parody if you want to be humorous) to bring your subject to life.

Just make sure the target audience will know the work you're parodying and that you don't change it so much that people don't recognise the original.

When Heinz was running the 'Any food tastes supreme with Heinz salad cream' campaign, they used the wolf from Little Red Riding Hood, lying in bed in granny's outfit, licking his lips. There was a bottle of Heinz salad cream by the bed… and no sign of granny.

17. Senses

We're working in visual media. But don't forget touch, taste, sound, smell. You can evoke them with your copy, and create a concept around that.

Or sometimes, you might be able to really use your audience's senses. And the more senses you can engage, the more immersive the work becomes.

In the Examples section of this book is a mailing I did that had a sound card in, which played distorted music when you opened it. Royal Mail once sent me a letter made of solid chocolate. And I once got a magazine insert where the stock was embossed to look – and feel – like old-fashioned vinyl wallpaper.

18. Play with the medium / format

We've already looked at this a bit in the Context section.

Bringing the idea to life through the medium or format is a very powerful, tactile and involving conceptual approach.

Just think: how can the subject, the benefit, product, problem or USP be demonstrated through the medium or format?

Augmented reality plays with the format. As do those billboards with things stuck on them. Or press ads that are scented. Or the ads on the side of buses that are lenticular. Or TV ads that have no picture, to make you focus on the sound.

Just because you've got a full page press ad space, doesn't mean you have to use it all. What if you just used a small portion in the middle, and left the rest as empty space? What kind of idea would that lead you to? Or what if, instead of one full page ad, you got the client to book two quarter page ads on consecutive pages? What idea could you come up with for that?

The poster for a health club that was a picture of a woman's torso, where the poster hadn't been pulled tight against the wall, so there was a real bulge in the poster... just where the woman's stomach showed between her gym top and shorts.

Or the doordrop for flexible, unbreakable glasses that asked you to try and rip open the envelope (but which used untearable Tyvek stock).

Or the Adidas viral that used your computer's IP address to make the Google Map in the ad show exactly where you happened to be when you were watching it.

19. Become another

Imagine how a completely different brand would tackle your subject. Or a famous person.

Become them. Think like them. Do an idea like them.

How would Honda do a McDonald's ad? How would DFS do it? Or Marks and Spencer? Or maybe, how could Stephen Fry sell McDonald's? Or Sly Stallone? Or Kate Moss? Or if it's a poster, imagine tackling it as a website brief. Or as a packaging brief.

20. Combine and refine

Look at the ideas you've come up with using any of the previous 19 techniques and try combining them.

Take your best ideas and see if any of them overlap, or could benefit from the best bits of each other.

You're not looking for a Frankenstein's monster, an ugly collection of bits that are obviously from different sources. But by taking the essence of one idea and using it to push on another that's not quite there, you could create something really original.

As long as it's simple and clear too, you've got the perfect vehicle for your scintillating copy.

ii. Style

We began looking at style back in 1.3 of this book, when we explored tone of voice and seven ways of being interesting. And then again in 2.2 when we examined brands.

But a captivating copywriting style is more of an art than a science. It's a heady combination of the brand, the concept, the tone of voice, you... and some indefinable bit of inspiration that anoints you while you're writing it.

That's one of the enjoyable things about copywriting. For all your preparation, for all that your experience and expertise guide you to what's 'right', every piece of copy still grows in its own way. You're the gardener, tending and encouraging it, but you still can't predict exactly how it will turn out. It will have a life of its own.

Often, the best thing is to write in a way that feels right at the time, and let the communication's individual style reveal itself. The more experienced a writer you are / become, the more natural this will feel. Then you can edit and rearrange the copy to make the style consistent and tweak the structure afterwards.

Of course, you'll also have your own voice which will seep into everything you write. Three things I'd say about that:

1. Don't *try* and develop your style – you won't need to, it will happen automatically.

2. Don't copy someone else's style. Many blogs, for example, try and copy each other's 'Hey, isn't everything shit' sarcastic drawl. If you copy someone else's style then you'll probably never be as good at it as they will be. And you'll never be as good at copying someone else as you will be at just being yourself. At best, you'll just be another 'me too' voice in the crowd.

3. Don't *try* and put yourself in the copy at all. You're not an artist, signing your own work. You're being paid to write copy that sells a subject to its audience. I only mention that the style of a piece will have a bit of 'you' in it because it's inevitable, not desirable.

So let me just repeat: the style of your copy will be an alchemical blend of what suits the concept, what suits the subject, the brand's tone of voice and your own tone of voice, plus the unique slant it gets from simply being that piece of copy written on that particular day to meet that specific brief.

History is littered with memorable examples of great copywriting. Yes, they were written by great wordsmiths who often had a distinctive style and who wrote other great copy. But somehow, those individual pieces we remember had a little magic of their own.

Every piece of copy you write has a chance to find its own unique voice. With you as the archaeologist using a soft-bristled brush, gently removing the soil to reveal the perfect outline of some Jurassic monster.

Michelangelo put it well.

He said that he didn't create statues like David. They were already there, in the stone. He simply chipped away the bits that weren't needed, to set them free.

---

iii. Structure

There's a Morecambe and Wise sketch where conductor Andre Previn says despairingly to Eric Morecambe (playing the piano in Previn's orchestra), "You're playing *all* the wrong notes."

Eric peers at him (irritably) through those thick-framed NHS glasses. There's a pause.

"I'm playing all the *right* notes," he snarls. Another pause. "Just not *necessarily* in the right order."

Structure's like that. It's there to make sure that what you write is in the right order.

Think of your copy as a series of segments. It's those segments you want to move around in order to create the strongest structure.

Handy hint

If you're writing very short copy you might not have many segments. In which case structure is probably irrelevant. It doesn't play a big part in billboards, for instance.

But aside from that, you should be able to go back over your first draft and segment your copy quite easily. The 'opening that builds on the headline' segment. The 'metaphor' segment. The 'main benefit brought to life' segment. The 'call to action' segment. The 'reprise of the opening' segment and so on.

Your copy may have different segments from those, of course. It may also have more. Or less. Which quickly demonstrates that *there is no universal 'best' structure.*

In fact, experimenting with structure is one of the ways you can be creative with copy and surprise (in a good way) your audience.

Now, to experiment with your structure and make it as engaging as possible, I recommend an approach I grandly call *The Song Method.*

Just create a list of your copy's segments, and think of each segment as the part of a song. A song might have an intro, verses, a bridge, a chorus, a guitar solo, a version of the chorus that goes up a key, a 'middle eight', an outro. And you could arrange those parts in many different ways.

'Intro, verse, bridge, chorus, verse, bridge, chorus, guitar solo, bridge, enhanced chorus, outro.'

That might be a typical kind of song structure. But it doesn't have to be like that. Plenty of good songs start with the chorus. Or have three verses before the first chorus. Many don't have a guitar solo of course. Some have two. Or three.

So: try rearranging your copy's segments and see which structure gives you the best combination of being both fresh and free-flowing.

I often have two or three documents open at once, all with the same copy. But in one I'll have the words in the original structure, in the others I'll try a couple of variations with the structure, moving the segments around to try it in different orders. Most times, it's one of these I'll end up using, rather than the more 'expected' structure of the original.

While you're experimenting, here are seven structure tips:

1. Don't have an 'introductory segment'. You'll have a first segment of course, but don't think of it like an introduction or you'll write something too soft and slow-paced.

2. Let the segments build on each other. A segment should move on from the previous segment, not a) jump around in time or b) seem completely unrelated. These are not a series of distinct subjects after all. This is one story divided into chapters.

3. Don't retrace your steps (apart from when you're deliberately making a reference from one segment to another). Otherwise, keep them quite discrete. Too much copy goes back and forth, repeating ideas from different segments. It makes it hard to follow, repetitive and sluggish. Be really disciplined about this.

3. Use a bit of word glue. In other words, when you're happy with the arrangement, make sure they link together seamlessly and feel like a flowing piece of copy. But don't use too much glue or you'll slow the story down. There are some examples of words that link sentences together in 3.22 of this book.

4. Considering your copy as segments is a great opportunity to do some pruning. Instead of just cutting words, could you cut segments? What's the least important segment? Could you lose it altogether, to give the rest more attention and prominence? Does every segment really have a strong role to play, or are some waffle or repetitious or tangents?

5. Remember AIDA from 1.3 – Attention, Interest, Desire, Action. While your copy doesn't need specific segments that do these jobs individually, AIDA is meant to be a chronological hierarchy, so consider whether or not your structure is helping you achieve that.

6. Make sure your best bits aren't buried. You're fighting a battle to win your audiences' hearts and minds – no point in waiting till late on, when the fight might already be lost. Look at where your best segments are – the big guns that are going to blow your audience away. Make sure they're near the front. Or, if they're late on, you should be utterly confident that the preceding segments draw the reader in so brilliantly, those big guns will still hit their target.

7. Fresh eye. Structure in particular is one of those areas which can benefit from having someone else read your copy. 'Can't see the wood for the trees' is an apt expression here: you can get so close to nurdling an individual sentence into perfection that you can lose sight of the fact that a quick bit of structural surgery could make a bigger difference.

And that's structure – the spine that holds your copy together.

Finding the best arrangement for your copy will really lift it, but sometimes people get very fixed ideas about what order you should tell the story in. You need to be open-minded to the idea that a communication's structure can be as individual as the copy itself.

For example

The film Gandhi. Starts near the end: with him getting shot. Then goes back in time 55 years, and the rest of the story is in chronological order, building up to repeating the scene where he gets shot.

By the way, the structure of this book changed many times. The number of chapters, the parts within those chapters, the order of those parts... all before we even get to the structure of each 'bit', like this one, where I've chopped things up more often than a supermodel's dealer. Allegedly.

Potent
psychological
triggers

Time for you to do voodoo.

To climb inside your audience's head. And mind. And brain.

In fact, we often talk of 'Head, heart and hand': persuade their head, move their heart and you'll get them to put their hand in their pocket to buy what you're selling (or do whatever else it is you want them to do).

And there are a number of psychological principles that will enhance the persuasive power of your copy.

Aside from any useful stuff I learned from taking a degree in psychology, it did also give me a lifelong interest in the subject.

I've continued to hoard snippets of insight into human psychology ever since. What makes us tick and the way we process information. It can all be used in marketing and advertising copy to make your story more compelling.

The result is a 'Dirty Dozen' of psychological triggers I'd like to share with you here. Well, they'd be a dirty dozen if you used your new powers for evil. You'll use them for good of course. Making them more of a 'Divine Dozen'.

These 12 psychological triggers are about how your copy can take advantage of the way we process information. Much like the way optical illusions take advantage of how we interpret visual information. (I'm always fooled by that one where the two lines are the same length, but look completely different according to whether the arrows on the ends point in or out.)

Some of the triggers overlap a little and they could be categorised differently from the way I've got it here, but I've always found these descriptions useful.

They're a fairly loose mix of cognitive psychology, developmental psychology, social psychology, pop psychology and pseudo-psychology that would have my lecturers turning in their corduroy-with-suede-elbow-patch jackets.

But hey, it's stuff that will make your copy more hypnotic than Paul McKenna.

Let the voodoo begin.

1. Popularity

It's this simple: people respond better to people they like than they do to people they don't like.

You'll do almost any favour for someone you fancy. The office bore who also happens to have poor personal hygiene?
Not so much.

Or imagine if a stranger tried to sell you raffle tickets.
Again, you're less likely to say yes than if a friend offered them to you. The prizes haven't changed. The charity that the money raised goes to hasn't become any more worthwhile. But because someone you know and like has offered the tickets to you, you're much more likely to say yes.

The same is true here. Write copy that makes people feel they know you and like you and they're more likely to do what you ask them to do.

Here are 10 things you might do to become liked by someone 'in real life' which you can easily replicate in copy:

i) Compliments / flattery

ii) Demonstrate shared interests / values / beliefs

iii) Show interest in them

iv) Be helpful

v) Mutual acquaintances

vi) Use the same kind of language (often done badly in copy)

vii) Be interesting

viii) Be successful

ix) Help them be successful (do something that makes them look good)

x) Familiarity (from having a strong brand they see regularly)

All are pretty self-explanatory; it's up to you how you use them in your copy.

It can start before you even write the copy. Imagine writing a mailing to a younger audience, for instance. They're so used to being bombarded online that a personally-addressed letter, sent through the post, stands out: it feels like someone's taking a special interest in them by writing.

Or something like 'mutual acquaintances' can be exaggerated by having the copy written by a celebrity the audience likes – they like him/her, so they'll like your product by association too.

One of the most famous opening lines in a direct mail pack was for American Express. It began, 'Quite frankly, the American Express Card is not for everyone. And not everyone who applies for Card membership is approved.' It's a great example of conveying exclusivity and of being subtly flattering by suggesting you might become part of this exclusive club.

For example

2. Consistency

You often hear people complain about being pigeonholed. Yet the truth is, we like to pigeonhole ourselves. Because it gives us a sense of identity. Who we are and who we're not.

We like to think of ourselves as being such-and-such a person with such-and-such a personality.

And to help that maintain that belief, we need to feel that we're consistent in our thoughts and actions.

If someone has bought from you before, they're a customer – a customer who clearly values great quality. Remind them of that. Make them feel good about the type of person they are and allow them to buy this new product from you, because it's clearly how they see themselves.

Brand 'fanboys' are an extreme example of this – people who see themselves as the type of person that the brand portrays their customers to be. So they'll buy everything the brand produces, whether good, bad or indifferent.

If you can get some insight into how the audience sees themselves (or would like to see themselves) then you can write about how your subject will help them continue to be that kind of person.

And if you know something they've done, you can use that to suggest that the action you now want them to take is consistent with what they've done before. Amazon does this after you put an item (let's call it X) into your shopping basket. The page reads 'People who bought X also bought Y and Z'.

'You're clearly someone who cares about our planet – and joining our campaign to stop rainforests being destroyed was a wonderful way to make a difference. That's why I'm sure you'll want to help again today, by forwarding the attached message to the Chief Executive of EvilCorps, which is still destroying 100 hectares of rainforest a day to...'

3. Conformity

One of the things that defines us is which groups we're part of and which groups we're not.

People perceive us differently according to which groups we belong to, and because we know that, we aspire to be in certain groups (and aspire not to be thought of as part of other groups) pretty assiduously.

In social psychology they call it 'ingroup / outgroup behaviour'. The 'ingroup' is one you think you belong to (or aspire to belong to). The outgroup is one you don't belong to (or at least, don't want to belong to). People's actions can be shaped by wanting to be part of a certain ingroup or separate from a certain outgroup – and you can use that trigger in copy quite easily.

Let's look at the copy about rainforests that I suggested for consistency, and change it slightly to use the ingroup trigger instead:

'Clearly, you're someone who cares about the destruction of the rainforest – and joining our campaign to stop rainforests being destroyed was a wonderful way to make a difference. That's why I'm sure you'll want to join the other people like you who took part in that campaign, by forwarding the attached message to the Chief Executive of EvilCorps, which is still destroying 100 hectares of rainforest a day to...'

Of course, you can combine more than one psychological trigger – you could use both *consistency* and *ingroup conformity* triggers by writing: 'I'm sure you'll want to help again today, like so many others who took part in that campaign are, by...'

Alternatively, the same basic copy could have used the *outgroup conformity* trigger instead.

'Clearly, you're someone who cares about the destruction of the rainforest – and joining our campaign to stop rainforests being destroyed was a wonderful way to make a difference. But today, we need to act again. I'm sure you don't want to be one of those people who stands on the sidelines, watching big business getting away with despicable acts of environmental rape. That's why I hope you'll forward the attached message to the Chief Executive of EvilCorps…'

Brands often have a big element of ingroup / outgroup triggers to them. Are you a PC or a Mac person? Marmite: you either love it or you hate it. And if you buy Armani jeans, you're unlikely to match them with a Matalan sweater.

Brands show you an 'ingroup' and say 'If you want to be part of this group, buy our product'.

Look at the brand you're working for: what would its ingroup look like? Its outgroup? Then you can use the conformity trigger to add a little gentle persuasion.

4. Credence

If David Attenborough told me they've discovered a population of orangutans in Borneo that are evolving into a brand new species of human, I'd believe him.

If my taxi driver said it, probably less so.

Credibility is very important in copywriting – you're trying to persuade someone, so it helps enormously if they think a) your trustworthiness is credible and b) your authority is credible.

The brand can help with both of those, as can copy that speaks in a confident tone and has detail that shows you know what you're talking about and have done since 1853.

Somebody else endorsing your subject can help your copy's credibility, which is why testimonials work. You're putting words in the mouth of someone else like the audience, saying they (for instance) bought the product and they're delighted with it.

It's why we look at the reviews on Amazon, to see what other people have said about that *Greatest Eurovision Hits… Ever!* album we're thinking of buying.

Awards help too. If there's an award associated with your subject, mention it. The audience won't know what the award is, won't know what the judging criteria were… yet it's still proven to add credibility to your subject.

5. Comparative mind

There are very few absolutes in the human mind. We judge most things by comparing them with other things.

Which means you can influence what people think about something by influencing what they compare it with.

Want to feel bad about your life? Think about the world's most popular, most successful rock star / film star and what their life must be like compared to yours. Want to feel good about your life? Reflect for a moment on a child born HIV+ in a poor African village.

Rolls Royce is a good example. If they have their £300,000 Silver Phantom at a car show, it probably looks a bit pricey compared to the others.

So what they often do is have them at boat shows. Where, if you're looking at a £4,000,000 yacht, picking up the world's most luxurious car seems like a snip.

And you'll sell more jeans costing £150 a pair if you also sell jeans costing £250 a pair – because by comparison, the £150 pairs will seem good value.

You can use our predisposition to compare things very effectively in copy.

If you're selling something expensive like a Roller, compare it with a yacht to make it seem relatively inexpensive.

If you're selling something cheap, like donating £3 a month to charity, compare it with how much less a month that might be than what they spend on take-away coffees. Suddenly £3 to save a life seems like nothing.

Compare the upside of having your product with the downside of not having it, to exaggerate its benefit.

Compare where your product is close to another in performance, but cheaper. Or, if you're dealing with something expensive, compare it to something cheaper but not as good.

Fairy washing-up liquid used to compare their product with the 'next best-selling brand' and demonstrate that it was better quality and so lasted 'up to 50% longer'. Which meant that although a bottle cost a bit more, it was actually cheaper per use.

Compare your new product with your old one: it's got 50 more horsepower, it lasts twice as long, it washes twice as clean, its graphics are 30% more powerful. This comparison with your own old stuff is amazingly effective, because it says either 'Didn't buy before? You were right to wait… the time to buy is now' or it says 'Bought our last product? It's out of date and you're behind the times… get the new one.'

Compare before and after. Compare the benefits of your subject with similar benefits in a completely different area.

Compare to contrast. To exaggerate. To borrow brand equity or feelings or attributes from another category. Compare to highlight benefits. Compare to downplay disadvantages.

6. Loss aversion

Every year in the January sales, people in the UK spend over £600 million on clothes they will never, ever wear.

Bought, taken home, put in a cupboard and *never* taken out.

Why? Because no-one likes to miss out. And when you're at the sales, among the crowds and people are jostling and elbows are flying and shelves are emptying, you get caught up in the moment. You get into a sales panic. 'If I don't grab something quick I'm going to miss out!'

So you buy something that later, you don't even want.

Lots of 'Sale Ends Tuesday', 'Limited Time Offer', 'Only a few remaining' stuff works on that basis.

And look at eBay: prices are often driven up by people getting into a frantic bidding war. It's not just that they want the item; they want to 'win' and not be the loser who misses out – even if that means they have to pay a premium to do so.

Near the end of a piece I wrote for a credit card; 'As I'm sure you understand, we expect this offer to be very popular. For that reason, we're unable to guarantee how long we will be able to make it available, even to specially-chosen customers like you. So if you do think this opportunity is right for you, please apply as soon as you're able, to avoid missing out.'

Of course, the brand you're writing for may not suit an 'everything must go' sales-y tone of voice. In which case, you can still use this psychological trigger of not missing out by conveying a little exclusivity.

7. Bargain

"It's a deal, it's a steal, it's the sale of the fucking century. In fact, fuck it – I think I'll keep it." So says Tom in the film *Lock, Stock and Two Smoking Barrels*.

Getting a deal or a bargain is closely related to loss aversion. In the case of the January sales, for example, it's a bargain that you're afraid of missing out on.

It doesn't have to involve loss aversion though; the feeling that you're getting a good deal is a powerful psychological trigger all of its own.

This doesn't mean you have to write copy that suggests your subject is *cheap*; instead it can simply be *good value*.

When a pricey perfume (sorry, *parfum*) throws in a free bag, suddenly it seems like a bargain. When a charity tells you that you can save a child's sight for just 80p, that sounds like great value. And when Sainsbury's gives you a bunch of vouchers, you feel you're getting a good deal on the things you buy with them; a feeling you wouldn't have got if the things had just been permanently at that lower price in the first place.

8. Mutuality

We're an awfully polite bunch, us humans. If someone smiles at us, we smile back.

And if someone does us a favour, we feel obliged to do them a favour back.

Somebody adds a link to your blog, so you add a link to theirs. Somebody writes a great recommendation of you on LinkedIn and then asks you to recommend them… you kind of have to, even if actually you didn't really rate them.

Give people things in your copy by telling them something interesting or useful. Entertain them. Make them smarter. Show them how to get a bargain.

Handy hint

Give them something for free and the mutuality gene kicks in: they'll be more inclined to do something for you. Like buy your product.

It might sound crazy, but humans are not rational beings. We're a bit mental when it comes to freebies.

For instance, have you ever had a charity mail pack with a pen in? Why do they do that? The pens are rubbish. Plus, you already have a pen. Several, in fact. So you don't need a rubbish one to fill out the donation form. And if you listen in on focus groups (as I have), you'll know that people who give to charities say time and time again "Don't send me a pen – I don't want it and it's a waste of money".

And yet, test two identical mail packs, one with a pen in and one without, and the one with the pen will get a better response. People feel indebted and give more. For being given a rubbish pen they didn't ask for and don't want.

9. Heuristic bias

Heuristics refers to the way we make decisions. It's an amazing area of social science and can be harnessed in copy to make it more persuasive.

One such heuristic bias is called *anchoring*, and here's an experiment example:

A group of people are asked to think of a random number and write it down. It can be any number they want. But first, a numbered wheel is spun, and the result is given to the group. They're told this is just part of the process and that they are to completely ignore the number, it has no relevance whatsoever.

Yet, if the wheel was giving very high numbers, the group 'randomly' came up with a high number. If the wheel gave a low number, the group came up with lower numbers.

They couldn't help but be influenced by the number, even though they knew it was randomly created and they were told to ignore it.

For persuasive copy, it's a goldmine. Here are three types of heuristic bias you can use:

i) anchoring

As in the experiment with the number wheel, this is the tendency to allow one piece of information to disproportionately dominate our decision-making.

Ever worked somewhere where the new recruit sucked? You can see it, everyone else can see it – hell, even the new recruit can probably see it.

But you know who'll struggle to see it? The person who hired them. Because that bit of information, 'I hired this person', disproportionately dominates their judgement. They hired the recruit, so the recruit must be good. Because if they weren't good, that would mean the person made a poor decision in hiring them. They can't admit that to themselves, so the fact that they did the hiring 'anchors' their thinking.

ii) availability

Information that stands out in some way seems more available – and is therefore more influencing.

For instance, knowledge of our own driving is more available than knowledge of other people's driving. We're closer to our own driving. The result is that around 80% of the population thinks their driving is 'above average'. Which of course it can't be. Since the average wouldn't then be the average.

In copy, you can make information more 'available' by putting it in a headline or a call-out box or side panel or subhead; that makes it more influencing (it's why there are so many rules in financial advertising about talking about the disadvantages right alongside the advantages).

A second, subtler way is to use words that relate in some way to the subject, without necessarily saying them *about* the subject. Ok, that sounds confusing – so try this on someone. Say to them, in turn, "Spell the word 'silk'. Say the word 'silk' three times. What do cows drink?"

People will very often say, "Milk". Much more often than if you just ask them, "What do cows drink?"

You can influence your audience in a similar way by using language that fits with the things you want the audience to think about your subject, even when you're not talking directly *about* your subject.

If you were writing about a product that you wanted to seem sexy, such as a perfume, then use sensual language throughout the copy, not simply to describe the product.

For example

Maybe the ad is about a woman getting ready for a night out, ending with using the perfume, but before that they take 'a slow, steamy shower' and 'slip into a sheer, silken dress that clings to every curve' and they bite into a 'velvety smooth Belgian chocolate' before applying their most 'seductive, irresistible lip gloss'. Simply the availability of these words makes the perfume seem sexier.

A third way of using the availability bias is 'misleading vividness'. This is where making something more vivid in someone's mind makes it feel more likely than statistically it is.

For instance, ever told someone you were thinking of buying product X, and they said "Oh, I know someone who had one of those, it broke after three weeks! Terrible."

That's pretty vivid available information, and it might well put you off buying the product. Because you've got some negative, first-hand available information on it. And you don't seek out the facts which show only 0.1% of people have ever had their product X break. Unlike product Y which you end up buying, which has actually broken in 1% of cases.

'It could be you'. Copy about winning the lottery makes the experience of winning seem very vivid, to the point where people talk about how'd they'd spend the money if they won. Yet… well, look at London. It's pretty big and rather busy. Yet if every single person in London bought a lottery ticket, each with a unique set of numbers, there's still around a 50% chance that not one of them would win the jackpot.

A fourth, very simple use of availability is the 'first and last' way our short-term memory works: when given a list of just about anything, people remember the first and last items better than any other positions. So in copy, make sure your important points (such as product benefits) are at the start and the end of your communication.

iii) risk aversion

This is the idea that people are more scared by risks than they are motivated by a similar gain. Usually, the potential gain has to massively outweigh the potential risk for people to go for it.

When presenting concepts, for instance, never refer to your dullest concept as 'the safe one'.

Because the trouble is, if that one's 'safe', it automatically positions the others as 'risky'. And according to the heuristic of risk aversion, we've effectively warned our clients off the more interesting work, because we've implied that it's risky.

Say you're writing a TV ad for home insurance. Instead of writing a voiceover that talks about gaining peace of mind, talk about how many people get burgled every year, how many house fires there are, how many houses suffer flood damage – all of which mean people can lose their most treasured possessions.

Of course, insurance doesn't stop you losing treasured possessions (it may be able to replace them), but this positioning of seemingly minimising your risk with the home insurance will be very powerful.

10. Emotional decisions

Have you ever seen *Deal or No Deal*? Perhaps not, I'll explain it.

Basically it's a game of random chance. There are a dozen or so shoeboxes. Each has an amount of money written inside, from about 50p to £100,000. The contestant gets given one of those boxes, but they don't know how much money is in it.

Each round of the game they choose three of the other shoeboxes to open, to reveal how money is written inside. When the amounts are revealed, they're crossed off the list of all the possible values, narrowing down the options of what's going to be in the contestant's shoebox.

After every round when the contestant has opened three boxes, the unseen 'banker' makes them an offer for their box. He doesn't know what's in it either, so basically he offers around the average amount of all the remaining values of the unopened boxes (sometimes slightly higher, sometimes slightly lower).

Say someone gets to the point where the banker offers them £46,000, an exactly fair offer based on the values remaining. But the contestant decides to play on and open another three boxes. They open ones which turn out to be most of the high value figures, meaning their box is more likely to have a low value. Damn, they've made a mistake. They should have accepted the £46,000 offer.

So now the banker makes a new offer: £21,000. Looking at the unopened values remaining, £21,000 is actually *higher* than the average. It's a generous offer. So the contestant should bite the banker's hand off and say yes. Walking away £21,000 richer just for having been on a gameshow for a day.

But they don't. The contestant isn't thinking about the 'generous' £21,000 offer. They're thinking about the £46,000 they were being offered just moments earlier. They feel stupid. They feel angry. And they see that there's still one £50,000 value still to be opened: maybe that will be in their box. Maybe they can still come out on top.

However, the odds are very much against them getting the £50,000. And in fact, after playing on for several rounds, they end up with just £200.

All because they had 'A rush of blood to the head'. They went from being rational and playing the odds to letting their heart rule their head and chasing the £46,000 prize they'd turned down.

It's why there are lots of references to emotive copywriting throughout this book: *because emotions are very powerful influencers of decision-making.*

What's more, our brains process information emotionally first, rationally second. It's an evolution thing: fight or flight. You need to know in a heartbeat whether to flood the body with adrenaline and fight the T-Rex or run from it. (Okay, I know there weren't any T-Rex's in human evolution. All the dragons had killed them.)

Which means that a) we can't help but process information emotionally, and b) emotions are powerful influencers. Put the two together and you can see why it makes sense to use emotion in every piece of copy you write.

There are two types of emotion to bear in mind.

First, the emotions that the brand wants their audience to feel. The emotion for Coke, for instance, is *innocent happiness*. Simple All-American perfect-smile happiness, without any edginess. Take another global American brand, Nike. There, the emotions are around personal and public achievement through sporting excellence.

For example

A classic Nike ad showed a basketball legend leaping high, about to slam dunk the ball. The line: Michael Jordan 1, Isaac Newton 0. Idea, image and line together stir the emotions – without using any emotive words.

Second, the universal emotions that your individual communication or campaign can leverage to influence the audience. These tend to be cruder, louder emotions than the subtleties of most established brands, so you need to use them carefully. But here, we're talking about 'negative' emotions such as *anger, fear, greed* and *guilt*, and 'positive' emotions such as *joy, love, achievement* and *fellowship*.

Of course, I'm not saying that you use those actual words – show, not tell. Stir the emotions and you'll stir me into action.

Remember, as mentioned in 1.4 of this book, audiences will also need the rational justification for the action we want them to take.

Handy hint

Not least because they need to rationalise to themselves and others why they took that action. And people aren't keen to admit it was 'Because the ad made me feel all gooey'.

11. Framing

This is the phenomenon that enables you to influence an audience's behaviour by the way you present the subject.

Comparisons and leading with the potential loss rather than the equivalent gain are psychological triggers in their own right, but they're also examples of framing – presenting the information in a certain way.

Aside from these two specific types we've already covered, framing is an area that often needs you to think laterally and find a new way to present an option to make it more compelling.

For instance, have you seen the 'Piano stairs' video on YouTube, part of 'The Fun Theory' for Volkswagen? On the underground in Sweden there's a set of stairs next to an escalator. And most people are using the escalator. So how do you re-frame the stairs, to make them a more attractive option?

They turned the stairs in a giant piano keyboard, complete with sounds when you stepped on them. And lo and behold, suddenly everyone wants to use the stairs. Giving them all a little extra exercise into the bargain.

As I say, every challenge has its own unique framing opportunities, so think about how your copy might re-frame the action you want people to take, to make it the most attractive option.

12. A smile in the mind

If you're happy, you're more likely to smile.

But weirdly, that wiring works the other way around too.
If you smile, just the mechanical action of smiling (even
without a reason) will often make you more happy.

It's this kind of feedback mechanism you can use in copy
to influence your audience. By giving them 'A smile in the mind'
for whatever reason, you make them feel more predisposed
to what you have to say.

For example

'"I never read the Economist." – Management trainee, aged 42.'
'Retire early with a good read.' 'What exactly is the benefit of the
doubt?' Remember those classic Economist ads?

There were hundreds of them and they were very witty. Sometimes they
gave you 'A smile in the mind' because they were amusing. And sometimes
they made you smile because they took a moment to work out, and when
you did, you felt pleased with yourself for having done so.

Make your audience smile (in a way that's relevant) and you're
halfway to having them sold.

As you can see, psychology in copywriting is a vast subject.
These 12 psychological triggers should be a useful start.

But if you want to know more about psychology or how we
can use the way our brains work to influence your audience
then I recommend *The Decisive Moment* by Jonah Lehrer,
Emotional Intelligence by Daniel Goleman, *Influence* by Robert
Cialdini, *Nudge* by Robert Thaler and Cass Sunstein, *Blink*
by Malcolm Gladwell, *The Happiness Hypothesis* by Jonathan
Haidt and *Introduction to Social Psychology* by Miles Hewstone
et al (one of my psychology lecturers from all those years
ago at uni).

Apparently, Mozart wrote music flawlessly, first time.
No mistakes, no amends.

He just put quill to parchment… and requiem after symphony
after concerto poured forth, each perfectly transcribed from his
head, without so much as a demi-semi-quaver out of place.

You, however, are no Mozart.

You'll have to work your way up to perfection, over a number
of iterations.

This is where, late into the night, you *craft that draft.*

The 'best' way to craft varies according to personal preference.
And by what kind of day you're having. And whether or not
the muse has caught you.

Some days your fingers will be a blur and you'll bash out
a decent draft very quickly. Other days you can agonise over
every punctuation mark, or which modal verb to use.

But whatever kind of day you're having, spending time to craft
your draft is what can make good copy great. The main thing
you'll need is perseverance.

Make your motto 'Good… is a good start'.

Review,
edit &
polish

Handy
hint

---

i. Review

Of course you'll want to review what you've done against
the brief, the proposition, the objectives, and whether or not
it meets the three corners of the context pyramid (brand,
audience and medium).

But I recommend you review it *in isolation* of all those things
first. Just review it as a piece of great (or not) copy.

Other people involved in the project will *immediately* review
your copy against every element on the brief – but that just tells
you if the copy meets the brief, not whether or not it's particularly
good. It's like when people proof-read: they check there are no
typos and that it makes grammatical sense. They're not checking
whether or not it's any good.

So: notice what you think works particularly well (or doesn't). How it seems overall. How it makes you feel. Whether or not anything leaps out as needing attention and *then* check back with the brief.

If your best copy seems at odds with elements of the brief, then you need to take an objective look at it: have you come up with a great line that isn't really relevant, or have you really found a better way of telling the story?

Handy hint

Make your copy better overnight. By leaving it overnight.

Always give your copy a read with 'fresh eyes' by coming back to it the next day and reading it anew. Sometimes it's not the total number of hours you have to work on a job that's important, it's having enough elapsed hours.

If you have one full day to write some copy, say eight hours in total, but it has to be done by the end of that day, the chances are that copy won't be as good as if you'd had eight hours spread over two days to work on the copy (say two sessions of four hours each).

Because in the hours between those two sessions, your brain will still be assimilating what you've done, thinking about it… and when you go back to it that second time, you'll read what you've done afresh and be able to improve it a notch or two quite easily.

Finally when reviewing, I think an important question to ask is 'Is this the way I always do it?'

In other words, we all have established patterns to our writing, a preferred approach. Like an old, favourite jumper. It may have a few bobbles and be wearing thin at the elbows, but it's comfortable and reassuring and we wear it far more often than we should.

If your copy has fallen into a routine (albeit a slick, effective one) then notice it when you're reviewing your copy. Realise that there were many other approaches you could have taken, and that you're in danger of falling into a rut.

Vow to challenge yourself more next time.

ii. Edit

And another thing: you've written too many words.

You verbose, rambling chatterbox.

Editing is the pruning of copywriting: cutting out what you don't need, finding ways to make everything clearer, sharper and shorter so your best lines aren't buried among weeds.

Partly it's a matter of finding dead-ends; half-formed ideas that distract from the main thought and can be done away with. And partly it's a matter of tightening up every single element.

Make your opening sentence 20% shorter. Lose a waffly paragraph. Re-write one long sentence with three commas into two sentences with no commas. Find a shorter word than 'remonstrate'. Use a more interesting word than 'nice'. Get to the action faster. Eradicate any repetition. Lose the bit you love but everybody else says doesn't work.

Sometimes I'll edit copy other people have written – say the Managing Director putting a new business proposal together.

For example

He'll write: 'Current messaging in the sector is bland and inconsistent and does little to tackle some of what we believe to be the barriers which prevent many people from acting. Much of this advertising also appears aggressive and 'selly' rather than nurturing or supportive which is perhaps surprising given the sensitivities of the subject of personal debt.'

I'll edit that to become: 'Most personal debt advertising is either bland or aggressive. It lacks the supportive tone that will engage your audience and doesn't address the four reasons that stop people from acting.'

Now it's a third shorter. It's got a more active voice. Shorter sentences. It gets to the point faster and in a clearer structure. And it's more specific, changing 'the barriers' to 'the four reasons' – and it moves this insight to the end of the para, so you're interested in reading the next para to discover what those four reasons are.

Of course, it's easy to be ruthless with someone else's copy. You've got to develop the discipline to be ruthless with your own.

Remember, make sure your writing isn't littered with flowery adjectives and adverbs. Go through it and start cutting them out; they're making your copy look amateurish and you as if you're trying too hard.

Incidentally, how many times can you use the word 'and' consecutively in a sentence so it still makes perfect sense and doesn't need any editing?

How about five?

Man walks into The Rose and Crown pub. "I like your new sign," he tells the landlord, "but there's a mistake."

"Really? What's that?" asks the landlord.

"The signwriter hasn't separated the words," the man replies. "So there's no gap between Rose and and and and and Crown."

Genius.

Now, sometimes good editing can make things longer. Because the purpose of editing shouldn't be simply to make things shorter. In short, it should be to make things simpler. And sometimes simpler copy takes a few more words.

Another Managing Director proposal: 'This proposal has been developed following an initial exploratory meeting on 29th March. It outlines how we recommend approaching and quantifying the most suitable target audience for an integrated campaign, what propositions work for these groups and creatively how they are best expressed.

The assumptions and costs provided within this document are based upon the initial discussion only and thus could vary slightly upon further exploration.'

I edited that to: 'This proposal shows how we can help you identify, reach and recruit the most valuable audience groups.

We had a very stimulating session together on 29th March – and we've used that meeting as a springboard. To make the most of the tremendous opportunities you have and to develop the most effective propositions into a creative, integrated campaign.

We've made some assumptions (including around cost) based on that meeting; obviously we can pin these down as we work together more closely.'

It's nearly 20% longer. But reads 100% better. And unlike the original, it leads with a clear promise to the reader – a benefit that encourages them to read on.

iii. Polish

Are you missing a trick?

A chance to make an element of your copy sparkle a little more brightly?

Because as well as reviewing and editing your copy to make it sharp, you should be making sure it is as *lively* as possible.

You'll have written it to be like that in the first place, of course. But it's possible that somewhere along the way, you lost a bit of impetus. Or you got worn down trying to shoe-horn everything in.

So some bits of copy are likely to be a little rougher and in need of a little spit and polish.

Light a match, drop it into the polish tin, put the lid on. The flame will liquefy the top of the polish and it'll buff things to a mighty fine shine.

Take a lesson from Elmore Leonard. Before he was an author, he was a copywriter. He also produced '10 rules for writing' which are worth looking up. The last one was 'If it sounds like writing, I rewrite it'.

Handy hint

To help with your polishing, bring back SOPHIE from the *Create* section. Useful for judging your concept, she's also very useful for reviewing the actual copy.

So, going through each in turn, how can you make your draft:

- simpler?
- more original?
- more powerful?
- more honed?
- more intelligent?
- more emotive?

When you've done that, you should be pretty pleased with what you've got.

But to ensure your copy is as lively as it can be, double-check what could be the 'Big Five' of your copy: *headline, opening, problem/solution benefit, visualization* and *call to action*.

1. Headline

Is your headline a particular 'type'?

For instance, does it convey: news; a benefit; a promise; an insight; a surprising / shocking fact? Does it make a command; ask an interesting question; convey an emotion; appeal to the reader's intelligence; or is it intriguing?

Know what type of headline you've got and you'll know how to polish it – by making it more so.

Handy hint

Your headline is probably the first thing your audience will read, but it doesn't have to be the first thing you write. While writing the headline first might help get you started, sometimes it can be better to write the body copy first, at which point a few headline candidates might reveal themselves.

The other thing to be mindful of is ensuring that it works with the image (if there is one) to 'complete the circle'. In other words, don't 'show and tell'. Don't have a headline that merely says what we're seeing. The headline and image should be incomplete individually – it's only together that they should make perfect sense.

Handy hint

'Drop the stop'. Look at your headings – do they have full stops? Some people believe full stops can reduce readership; people get to the end of the headline, see the full stop and stop reading because the idea is complete. No full stop suggests you need to read on to get the whole story.

2. Openings

Openings are the bit you'll probably spend more time polishing than anything else. Rewriting it until it links from the headline perfectly, builds on it adroitly, and draws the reader into the rest of the copy beguilingly.

The best advice I can give you here is, just because you're only polishing – tinkering with your copy – doesn't mean your opening only needs a word change here and there. As we covered in *Structure*, you may have a killer paragraph halfway down the copy. What if you moved that to the very top, and then re-arranged the rest around that? Would that be a more powerful opening?

Alternatively, if your opening is looking a little prosaic, here are six commonly used opening techniques:

i) Conceptual

An opening that develops the concept that the whole communication is wrapped up in.

ii) Tease

Hint at something to come, before then changing the subject.

iii) Challenge

Either a slightly confrontational sit-up-and-take-notice beginning, like 'Why you're wasting £150 a year on life insurance that doesn't protect you' or a direct ask, like 'Want rock-hard abs in six weeks, without having to go to the gym?'

iv) Promise

Allude to a benefit to the reader straight away – even if it's only the implied promise that they're going to enjoy reading your communication, but more often the promise of a great benefit from your product / service / offer.

v) Aside

Like AA Gill's restaurant reviews, which open with a seemingly irrelevant topic.

vi) Personal

Either a personal experience from the writer or something personal about the reader, such as the famous opening by Bill Jayme for *Psychology Today:* 'Do you close the bathroom door, even when you're the only one home?'

There are a hundred other ways of opening your copy of course (including the ones mentioned earlier for headlines, such as news, shocking fact, question etc). The six above are just suggestions – build up a list of your own, and consider them at the polish stage as new ways to approach your opening line / paragraph.

3. Problem / solution benefit

Think about how you can polish up the problem / solution element of your copy. It's perhaps an old-fashioned way to think of things, that we're putting the spotlight on a customer 'problem' that our subject will 'solve'; but it's a very useful starting point for being clear about a benefit you can bring to the reader's life. Even a luxury, lifestyle item can be positioned in this way.

For example

To use Apple once more, think of the iPad. What problem might it conceivably meet? How about a customer who's thinking, "I want a computer that's really portable, something that looks good and is slick to use so I'll feel good about using it in public. And I want it for surfing the net and watching video, but not writing for long documents. So I don't really want / need a netbook... what's the alternative?" Think of it like that and you can have a very strong problem / solution benefit element in your copy.

When polishing your problem / solution content, concentrate on making them as:

    i) specific as possible

    ii) dramatic as possible (not to the point of incredulity)

    iii) relevant as possible (relevant to the audience)

    iv) provable as possible (with facts / examples / case studies backing up the proof of your solution).

4. Visualisation

Paint a picture with words. When polishing your copy, ensure your words are as evocative as possible. Nudge the reader into creating a picture... a scene... a whole world, in their mind's eye.

A great turn of phrase, an inspired metaphor, the occasional poetic flourish, onomatopoeic words – all of these can help your audience visualise your subject more powerfully. And the more they're becoming mentally involved, the more of their imagination you're engaging, the more involved they're becoming *full stop.*

And the more you've got them.

5. Call to action

You may not have a specific, expressed action that you want the reader to take, but if you have, a little polish here can make a big difference. For instance, consider:

  i) Have you said what you want the reader to do the right number of times? Mentioning it every other sentence might be too many. Only mentioning it once at the end might not be enough.

  ii) Have you made it as clear and unequivocal as possible? Is it absolutely apparent what you want the reader to do?

  iii) Have you made it as easy as possible to act and given enough options (or at least the method of acting that suits the target audience best)?

  iv) Have you conveyed some sense of movement, that they should act promptly?

  v) Does everything build towards making them feel good about acting?

And finally: be brave.

Polishing is your last act before the copy is pulled from your trembling, reluctant fingers. So it's your last chance to make sure that what you're handing over is a gift-wrapped example of great copy.

For instance, if you're having trouble polishing your copy, then maybe – just maybe – it's because what you've done is spectacular and beyond improvement.

Or it may be just unsalvageably bad.

It probably feels late in the day – but if when you're trying to polish your copy you realise it just isn't working, then start again afresh.

One new draft now, written quickly – but benefiting from all the thinking and practice you've already done – will probably give you better copy then trying to tinker with something that just doesn't seem to be working.

Because as everyone knows: you can't polish a turd.

Okay then master wordsmith – let's have a look at some *Quick Tips* and then onto some *Examples*.

3

Twenty-five top tips

3.1 Start with a short one

3.2 Features tell, benefits sell

3.3 Avoid clichés

3.4 Be unusual

3.5 Metaphors, similes and analogies

3.6 Hardwired words

3.7 Wax lyrical

3.8 Solutions not problems

3.9 Nouns beat adjectives

3.10 Avoid talking about cost

This is the little stuff; a grab bag of copy tricks and techniques that only take a moment to learn and which can improve your writing at a moment's notice.

To demonstrate how they can make an immediate impact, here's a five minute flipchart exercise I sometimes show clients. On the board I write the headline:

A few techniques to minimise the shortcomings in writing designed to persuade.

Then I say, tip one: make your writing active and personal. By saying things like 'your writing', for example. Write as one individual talking to another individual.

So, I make a change to the headline on the flipchart. It now reads:

A few techniques to minimise the shortcomings in *your* writing designed to persuade.

Second tip: use 'hardwired words'. There are words that just seem to get people's attention and interest, almost as if they're hardwired in our brains. One example is the word 'guaranteed'. Another is 'secrets'. They're potent, powerful words. So the headline now becomes:

A few *secrets* to minimise the shortcomings in your writing designed to persuade – *guaranteed*.

Third tip: be specific not generic. People like precision, facts, numbers, statistics. And the more tangible those are, the better. So instead of 'Save up to 40%', it's more effective to say 'Save as much as £65'. The headline gets another tweak:

Six secrets to minimise the shortcomings in your writing designed to persuade – guaranteed.

Fourth tip: talk about solutions, not problems. People buy solutions, they don't like hearing about problems. So, in an anti-dandruff shampoo ad where they have one big picture, it'll never be a picture of the problem. It'll be a picture of someone with dazzling, flake-free hair.

So the headline gets another couple of nurdles:

Six secrets *which can make* your writing *irresistible* – guaranteed.

Penultimate tip: features tell, benefits sell. So, when you get a credit card, 'Fraud protection' is a feature, while 'You can feel safe when you shop online' is the benefit.

The changes we've made to our headline have already made it more benefit driven, but we can enhance it further. Firstly, by putting the definite article at the beginning. And secondly by being bolder and saying the benefits 'will' rather than 'can'. We'll also add an important, new benefit: that these secrets are 'easy'. So now we have:

racket *The* **six** *easy* **secrets which** *will* **make your writing irresistible – guaranteed.**

Sixth and final tip: make your writing lyrical and lively. Use slightly unusual language, a little alliteration, a metaphor, onomatopoeia or a play on words to make it stand out.

We can make the headline more alliterative by changing 'easy' to 'simple'. And we can make it more distinctive by adding a punchy adjective:

The six *simple* secrets which will make your writing *bloody* irresistible – guaranteed.

And there it is. A new headline that means the same thing as the first one, but which is more engaging and effective, without being a single word longer.

Now let's look at twenty-five tips to turbo charge your technique.

As you can see, the alliteration can get a bit addictive.

3.1 Start with a short one

Almost always.

Whatever the medium, I almost always begin with a short paragraph.

Usually a short, single sentence, as you'll see in the *Examples* section of this book.

One reason is that when someone glances at your copy, just a glance will be enough for their brain to process a short, standalone line. And if that first sentence is interesting, they'll start to be drawn into your copy.

However if your opening copy is a dense block of unbroken text, like a four line paragraph, then a glance won't be enough to take it in. And you've lost a small but significant opportunity to engage your reader.

Your first sentence can be like a second chance at a headline – a bite-size morsel to whet their appetite and make them want to continue.

A second reason is that as well as *actually* being easier to take in, it *looks* easier to take in. It doesn't look like an off-putting wad of words. And it starts you off with the discipline of having some short, pithy paragraphs.

Like this one.

3.2 Features tell, benefits sell (& outcomes do well)

In the words of legendary copywriter John Caples: don't sell the world's best grass seed, sell the world's best lawn.

The feature is a characteristic of a product / service / offer.

The benefit is what that characteristic does for you.

The outcome is what your world is like as a result of that benefit.

Businesses are closer to their own products and services than their customers are. As a result, as well as often talking in jargon or technical terms without realising it, they can become convinced of the importance of every feature of that product or service.

But to persuade someone to buy, we've got to tell them about the benefits or outcomes that will most appeal to them.

Just listing the feature means you're asking the audience to work out what the benefit is for themselves – which they may not do. And even if the benefit is obvious, it'll sound better when brought to life by you.

For example

'Our new handbag comes in four great colours' is a feature; 'Four great colours means you can choose the handbag that matches your outfit' is the benefit; 'You'll turn heads everywhere you go' is the outcome.

3.3 Avoid clichés

Avoid clichés and tired, overused phrases. As I've mentioned before, 'peace of mind' has become a cliché for describing the benefit of any kind of insurance.

'I'm writing to you today' is one you still see in letters. They know you're writing to them, so telling them something they already know is a poor opening. Using a cliché to do it is even worse.

As a matter of fact, before you know it, what you'll find is, fate worse than death, push the envelope, best-laid plans, it's not rocket science, with the best will in the world, more affordable than you think, there is a better way to…

These phrases lose their meaning. So the audience doesn't really take in what you're saying. It also makes your writing seem bland. If your writing is bland, your message is bland, so your product or service seems bland by association. So maybe I don't want it.

And while we're at it, avoid jargon too.

'Fiscal drag' is one I heard the other day. Do you know what it means? It means the government keeps the tax bands the same, but over time people's earnings increase – so more people fall into higher tax bands, raising more tax income for the government, without it seeming like they're raising taxes.

Which is, admittedly, a drag.

3.4 Be unusual

Flabbergasted. Cock-a-hoop. Blabbermouth. Shonky. Obstreperous. Salubrious. High falutin'. Vituperative. Flim flam.

A huge fat wad of cash. A rare old time. A big beaming grin. A teensy weensy slice. Finger lickin' good.

Words or phrases with a bit of personality, that stand out from the crowd, can make your copy more memorable.

Even if people don't know the exact meaning of the word, they'll get the idea if it's in context.

Because, although we want our copy to be easy to read, we don't want it to slide straight off their eyes. We need a little friction for their brain to rub up against.

A moment's pause, courtesy of some striking language, will mean they're spending more time soaking up your copy. Which is good.

Novelists and poets often do it; describe something in an unusual (but evocative) way to really bring an idea to life.

What we looking for is the *opposite* of a cliché.

You can also use uncommonly-used words to 'own' an idea – what company does 'exceedingly' make you think of? You can probably remember their whole strapline – not because it's a great line, not because the ads are great, not because their cakes are so delicious… but because Kipling used a distinctive word. (The same distinctive word, in every ad.)

If you want to be really distinctive, make the word up. Shakespeare did. He invented hundreds of words that we still use today. Including, appropriately, the word *articulate*. According to my spellcheck there are a few made-up words in this book: blandathon, burpy, nurdle.

Many ads are remembered for the catchy phrases they coined – the one I remember from my yoof was 'Hello Tosh, got a Toshiba?'

Although my prize for best made-up word sequence would go to Pepsi for *Lipsmackin' thirstquenchin' acetastin' motivatin' goodbuzzin' cooltalkin' highwalkin' fastlivin' evergivin' coolfizzin' Pepsi.*

That was back in 1973. Time you came up with something to topple it.

3.5 Metaphors, similes and analogies

As I said in the *Concept* part of 2.3 of this book, metaphors can make good concepts, but not always.

The problem is they require the audience to translate the metaphor into the thing you're actually talking about. Which audiences often won't do if they're not paying attention. However, a metaphor (or simile or analogy) can definitely enliven your copy – in three ways.

First, the metaphor can bring an interesting new subject into your copy.

Second, the metaphor can be a clever comparison with the original subject which beguiles the audience.

And third, it can help the audience understand the point you're trying to make about the original subject.

King of the metaphor / simile, Jeremy Clarkson on describing a family car he finds surprisingly invigorating: "Think of it as a librarian with a G-string under the tweed."

The simile (a librarian in a G-string) is interesting, the comparison is clever and unexpected (and therefore interesting) and it's a simple, more interesting way to convey as ordinary a point as 'Doesn't look exciting but underneath it actually is'.

Here's another of Jezza's, this time about the (apparently unnecessary) suspension-adjustment lever on a Bentley: "It's about as useful as putting a snooze button on a smoke alarm".

He could have just said, "It's about as useful as a chocolate teapot", but that old simile has become a cliché – very tired and well past its use-by date. Instead, he came up with something clever and new that added life and meaning to his copy.

Here's Charlie Brooker, being somewhat unkind about Cilla Black: "She's starting to resemble the result of an unholy union between Ronald McDonald and a blow-dried guinea pig". Or Howard Marks, describing himself: "When I look in the mirror.... I see a not-too-recently excavated mummy of Mick Jagger."

Of course, you can be metaphorical in a less explicit way.

In the previous tip, talking about unusual words / phrases, I wrote, "Because, although we want our copy to be easy to read, we don't want it to slide straight off their eyes. We need a little friction for their brain to rub up against."

For example

Words aren't going to literally slide off their eyes, or literally rub up against their brain. It's a little metaphorical device, to illustrate the point.

3.6 Hardwired words

For some reason, some words are proven to get people's attention more effectively than others.

If you use one of those words in a headline, for example, there's more chance of it being read than if you don't. But remember 'relevant abruption' in the *Fantastic Four* section. Only grab attention in a way that's relevant.

Some of the words that seem to be hardwired into our brains and command our attention include:

Free	*Enjoy*	*Save*	*Win*
Now	*New*	*News*	*Thank you*
Guaranteed	*Discount*	*Limited time*	*Last chance*
Introducing	*Urgent*	*You*	*Secret*
Promise	*Cash*	*Prize*	*Rich*
Sex(y)	*Breakthrough*	*Proven*	*Discover*

And of course, using your reader's name always has the power to grab their attention (one reason so many spam emails do it). In fact, I've seen email testing which shows that having the recipient's name in the subject line significantly increases the open rate.

Using the name of a current celebrity works too – that's why so many newspapers and magazines run 'non-stories' about celebs, because just using their name increases sales.

See if you can discover more 'hardwired words'. (David Ogilvy claimed 'Darling' was one he'd found increased response when he added it to an ad's headline.)

3.7 Wax lyrical

Even if we have to say the same thing as everyone else, to the same people as everyone else, we don't have to say it in the same way as everyone else.

Take advantage of the richness of the English language to create rhythm, a little poetic flourish and the occasional moment of wordplay.

An article I wrote used both sour and sweet in their non-literal senses together: 'And walking onstage to pick up an award while fellow creatives clap sourly is a particularly sweet moment.'

Why is a light touch of wordplay important, rather than a self-serving waste of time? Well, it makes your copy more interesting to read. More distinctive. And more memorable. And so by association, the subject.

In other words, as long as you're being lyrical in a way that's appropriate for the brand's tone of voice, a little wordplay can be A Good Thing. Just, as I've mentioned before, be wary of falling in love with your own cleverness and indulging in wordplay that obscures or overwhelms rather than enhances.

Here are 20 alphabetically-arranged ways to be more lyrically lovely:

1. *alliteration* – words that begin with the same letter / sound. A pair of words together, as in 'dirty dozen' adds emphasis, but you can also use alliteration where the alliterating words don't appear together at all, but dispersed through a sentence, for a subtler effect. I saw one the other day: *Fantastic tasty Thai*. (They were referring to food. I think.) At first it looks like just the last two words alliterate, but actually, it's five syllables in a row: tast-tic-tas-ty-thai.

2. *antanagoge* – putting a plus next to a minus. It can be really useful in copy where you have to let the reader know about a disadvantage, for instance, 'Of course, it costs a little extra. But you'll save many times the price difference in just a year.'

3. *antimetabole* – where you repeat the same phrase, but reverse the order, as in 'Ask not what your country can do for you, ask what you can do for your country.'

4. *antiphrasis* – being ironic in a single word (like saying 'It's a *cheap* 10 million quid'). This kind of twist draws attention to the idea, to stick in the reader's mind.

5. *antithesis* – an example is 'One small step for a man, one giant leap for mankind'. It just means to compare two ideas, to put them together to contrast them. Lots of aphorisms (wise sayings) are structured in this way.

   (Incidentally, Neil Armstrong fluffed his lines – he said "One small step *for man*, one giant leap for mankind", missing out the indefinite article 'a'. So what he said was actually a contradiction, since 'man' and 'mankind' meant the same thing.)

6. *diacope* – repetition of a phrase or word, but with other words in between. 'Magnificent, it really is magnificent – in fact, the most magnificent example I've ever seen' for instance.

7. *dirimens copulatio* – 'But wait – there's more!' That's an example of dirimens copulatio in copy; amplifying an argument by building the story in a 'not only, but also' kind of way. As TV detective Columbo would have put it, "Just one more thing…"

   It can be very effective, if rather cheesy. Just flick to any of the TV shopping channels and see how they build the benefits of a product.

   The classic iteration is where they sell the benefits, tell you the price, you think that's the whole deal, it sounds pretty good but you're not quite persuaded… and then the 'But wait – there's more' moment arrives. They tell you that when you order today, you'll also get two for the price of one. Plus these three great accessories. Free delivery. And a free unicorn.

   Maybe you can find a subtle, sophisticated way to use the same principle.

8. *exemplum* – just means to use an example. This book is full of examples and they're useful in most forms of copy. Not only do they make your story more interesting, they can act as an illustration of your subject that's far more compelling, because you're making it real.

9. *hyperbole* – pronounced 'hi-per-bo-lee' (not 'hyper-bowl' as you sometimes hear), it refers to lyrical exaggeration.

   You can do it in a crude way, like, 'The most incredible sale the world has ever seen!' (hyperbole of that kind usually has exclamation marks, or 'screamers' as they're also called).

   Or you can do it more subtly, such as with an exaggerated metaphor like 'We were so poor, my parents got married just for the rice.' Or just by choosing descriptions that are more evocative and aspirational.

   Be careful though – hyperbole can become 'overselling' and make all your copy seem disingenuous and insincere.

The other day I was on a plane and the in-flight meal menu referred to 'homemade roast potatoes'. That didn't impress me, it just struck me as ridiculous. How can airplane food be homemade? In whose home? The pilot's?

That kind of overboard exaggeration just undermines your whole communication. And don't scatter meaningless adjectives everywhere. The occasional superlative can make a noun stand out, but if everything is 'fantastic', 'amazing' or 'incredible' then those words lose all meaning.

10. *hypophora* – asking a question and then answering it. Often useful since your audience is likely to have questions about your product / service / offer, so you can ask those questions yourself, then answer them. For example, 'What if you change your mind? Well, that's why we offer a 30 day money-back guarantee.'

11. *mis-saying* – changing a well-known or common expression slightly. For a watch ad, the headline 'There's no present like the time', reverses the 'There's no time like the present' expression.

    Reverse words or just change one of the words to another that rhymes with it or sounds like it – the less you change the better, so there's more chance people will get the original reference.

12. *onomatopoeia* – words that sound like the thing they describe. It's an interesting idea, since we're talking about copy that is unlikely to be read aloud – yet the way your words would sound out loud can still make a difference.

    Examples of onomatopoeia include buzz, zip, screech, whirr, crush, sizzle, crunch, bang, pow, zap, fizz, burp, roar, growl, blip, click, whimper and echo. In fact, onomatopoeia has been the whole premise of an enduring ad campaign – Rice Krispies' *Snap, Crackle & Pop*.

13. *oxymoron* – a contradiction in terms. The cheeky example often used is 'military intelligence'. You might use a contradiction in terms to make a comparison or draw attention to a particular point. 'Deafening silence' and 'open secret' are oxymoronic phrases.

14. *parallelism* – this just means repeating your linguistic structure in a phrase, sentence or paragraph. It creates a poetic rhythm to your copy.

    Here's an example from Cormack McCarthy's *The Road*, using parallelism to build up a sequence of actions with a sequence of nouns: 'He pulled the blue plastic tarp off of him and folded it and carried it out to the grocery cart and packed it and came back with their plates and some cornmeal cakes in a plastic bag and a plastic bottle of syrup.'

    There are many ways you can use parallelism. For instance, instead of different numbers of adjectives before each noun, as in "a book, a yellow pencil and a worn, dirty coat", you could consistently always have one, as in "a heavy book, a yellow pencil and a dirty coat".

15. *personification* – is where you give something that isn't human (usually an object), human qualities (such as emotions, senses, actions). So it can be as simple as 'Our new car just *begs* to be driven' or 'Milk's *favourite* cookie' (a strapline for Oreos) or 'Give your radio *a reason to live*' (a headline for Virgin radio).

    Perhaps one of the reasons personification works well is that we're obsessed with ourselves, so anything that's made more human is brought closer to us, made more real for us.

    A further exaggeration is anthropomorphism, where you give an animal the mind, emotions and even voice of a human. Like those 'charming' TV ads for a dog charity where the voiceover is supposed to be from the dog you're seeing on screen.

16. *pleonasm* – is to deliberately use word redundancy; normally we 'eschew surplusage' as Mark Twain wittily put it, but sometimes repeating an idea, perhaps with different words, can help.

    Not only does it create a rhythm, it may be that one way of expressing the idea appeals to some people, and another way appeals to others. Or, it may just create emphasis, as in 'The latest version is faster, quicker, more rapid' (which is not only an example of pleonasm, but of the power of threes too).

17. *pun* – another one, like hyperbole, that tends to be overused, especially by more junior writers. But don't *write them off* (there's a pun for you) – in the right hands, they can be awesome.

Let's say there are good puns and bad puns. In fact, good puns I just call 'wordplay', as 'pun' tends to be used as a derogatory term.

Puns are supposed to be (mildly) humorous or witty, so they only suit copy where that's appropriate. A pun is typically either:

a) deliberately using a word in a way where it could have more than one meaning, or

b) using a word that sounds similar to the word you'd normally expect in the phrase.

An example of the first type is by Charles Saatchi, who claimed his favourite of his own ads was for a haemorrhoid cream, with the headline 'How to lick your piles'.

The English language is replete with words that have two (or more) meanings, so there's always a lot of opportunity for wordplay of this kind.

An example of the second type, one that still makes me laugh for its sheer charming silliness, was the name of a scuba shop I once saw on holiday – 'Scuba Dooby Doo'. But my personal favourite of all time was (allegedly) an ad by an Irish company called Sofa King. Their strapline? 'It's Sofa King Good.'

18. *rhetorical question* – unlike hypophora, this means asking a question which you *don't* answer.

'Who doesn't love a rhetorical question?' That's one right there.

'Do you want thicker, shinier hair?' might be a useful example for a shampoo ad, where the target audience would, internally, be saying yes. But to avoid people saying 'No' and dismissing your copy, consider *open questions* (ie ones with lots of possible answers, like 'What does your favourite colour say about your personality?') instead of *closed questions* which can be answered 'yes' or 'no'.

19. *rhyme* – it may seem trite, but rhyme is a great memory aide.

    The Appliance of Science (Zanussi), O2 See what you can do, School fuel (Shreddies), Beanz Meanz Heinz or The flavour of a Quaver is never known to waver for instance.

    Most song lyrics rhyme of course – because it makes them more catchy and memorable. And similarly, don't we want our communication to be memorable?

    For inspiration, there are plenty of online rhyming dictionary sites that let you type in a word and find all the words that rhyme with it (or use assonance for a near rhyme).

20. *tautology* – means a phrase which contains an unnecessary repetition of meaning. 'Free gift' is the classic example. Because if something is a gift, then of course it's free. Otherwise it wouldn't be a gift. Yet it's often used because it just sounds stronger than simply saying 'free'.

    'I saw it with my own eyes' is a kind of tautology too. Of course you saw it with your own eyes – you're not likely to see it with someone else's, are you?

3.8 Solutions not problems

Usually, it's more successful to talk about the solution rather than the problem.

The example I mentioned in the flipchart exercise at the start of this section was anti-dandruff shampoo. Sometimes they can do a 'Before and after' that shows first the problem (dandruff), then the solution (shiny, 'flake-free' hair).

But in a space where they're leading with one main picture, it won't be of someone with dandruff. The picture will be of someone (a woman, usually) with glossy, beautiful hair. The outcome.

Straightforward testing, like for like, just shows that solutions outpull problems.

For example

For example: instead of 'Do you suffer from…(the problem)' try 'Wouldn't you love to have…(the solution)'

Although as always, it's not an absolute rule. It's often more creatively interesting to bring the problem to life rather than the solution, and a headline that leads on the problem certainly can work as it helps the target audience realise you're talking to them.

Just ensure that, if you do lay on the problem a bit thick, you leave some copy to talk about the solution.

3.9 Nouns beat adjectives

Ever read any Ernest Hemingway?

As I've said elsewhere, he wrote very sparingly. Not too much description. Very tight, focussed writing.

The advantage for copywriters of writing 'sparsely' by editing out some of your long-winded description is that you can get the 'meat' across more quickly, cutting out the fat.

It might also mean you let the reader do more of the imagining (which involves them more) rather than spoon-feeding them every detail.

But there's another point about nouns and adjectives – many ideas can be expressed as either a thing (a noun) or a characteristic of that thing (an adjective). And it's more powerful to express something as the noun, rather than the adjective.

So if you really want to convey expertise, 'our expert staff' is not as potent as 'our staff of experts'.

3.10 Avoid talking about cost, buy, price, pay, spend, owe

All of the words above are negative. They're bad things to have to put in your writing.

Why? Because they tell your reader that they're about to become poorer – which is always a bad thing.

So minimise their use – in fact, try not to use them at all.

Instead, try something like 'Yours for just £XX.99'. Or for something pricey, try 'invest' instead of buy – because investing is a positive thing.

If possible, you should even avoid using 'spend' even in a non-financial sense, because it always has monetary connotations, even when you don't mean it that way. So don't say 'Spend two nights at this luxury hotel'. Instead, simply 'Enjoy two nights at this luxury hotel'.

Avoiding using the *word* 'price' doesn't mean you should avoid *having* the price in your work. If you want someone to buy something, you must tell them how much it is. Just don't refer to it as a cost.

There's evidence that people won't pursue buying something if they don't know how much it is – they're put off by the idea that they might have to enquire, then discover it's too expensive and feel embarrassed.

3.11 Quantify

Another point made in the flipchart exercise at the start was how people prefer hard numbers when describing amounts. Even if those numbers don't really mean much to them, the idea that you're being definitive is effective.

Lots of copywriting is littered with phrases like 'some' or 'lots of people' or 'a number of' and so on – often simply because the writer didn't bother to find the actual numbers.

Instead of saying 'thousands of people have discovered…', use '15,000 satisfied customers have discovered…' Using a hard number just seems more powerful. The exception is when the actual number is very disappointing. Clearly you wouldn't want to use it in that case.

A final point to mention with quantities is how the language around them can affect the perception of that quantity.

 *If you want to make an event seem more likely, say 'you may win' rather than 'you might win'. 'May' feels more likely than 'might'.*

'Should you need to make a claim' is less likely than 'If you need to make a claim' (therefore, if you want people to think they're unlikely to need to claim, better).

'As much as' means the same as 'up to' but sounds bigger, because it has 'much' in it.

So car insurance ads on the TV shouldn't say 'Save up to 40%', they should say 'Save as much as 40%'. Actually, they should give the amount in pounds – it should be 'Save as much as £120'.

And don't say '20% off', say 'Save 20%'.

3.12 Be active not passive

An active style means using 'you' and 'I' and 'they' in copy so that it's clear who we're talking about. A passive style loses this and creates distance between the topic and the reader. The only example I can think of where this is done deliberately is insurance booklets, where instead of saying 'if you have an accident' they'll say 'in the event of an accident'.

But, unless you're writing insurance booklets, avoid this passive style. As I've said elsewhere, particularly consider having plenty of 'you' and 'your' in your copy.

3.13 Keep it short. Or long.

Whatever the medium, you'll always have people telling you to make what you've written shorter.

But we're writing to persuade someone to do something which they would not do otherwise. Which sometimes needs more words. Here are my two rules for copy length:

Copy should never be longer than the space it suits.

Copy should never be longer than you're capable of being interesting for.

The first point is one of simple logistics: you can't pour a quart into a pint pot.

It's all very well thinking that every word you've written is sublime, but if you write more than the space you're working in can comfortably house, then it'll look awkward and off-putting and no-one will read it. And don't settle for squeezing in the most it can possibly carry either; edit and trim your copy until it looks relaxed and elegant in situ.

The second point is more about persuasion. Basically, it takes time to persuade someone to do something (especially if it involves them in parting with cash and especially if you approached them rather than the other way around).

So to a certain extent, the longer you can spend with your prospect, convincing them of your argument, the more chance you have of persuading them. To use another well-worn aphorism 'The more you tell, the more you sell'.

That's why there are companies offering a free holiday, provided you agree to come to a three hour talk on timeshares.

Because they know that if they can present their case over three hours, you're much more likely to be persuaded.

It's why a good car salesman will strike up a conversation with you, explore what you're interested in and really go to town on why such-and-such a car is perfect for you. Because the more he talks, the more you're persuaded.

All of which suggests that long copy may be more effective than short copy, in whatever medium you're trying to persuade in. Which begs the question, why is so much copy so short nowadays, with clients pleading for the copy to be shorter still?

One reason may be that the copy just isn't very good.

Because it's fine to write 100 lines of copy (assuming you have the space) if all 100 lines are interesting.

If you can write a compelling first sentence, your audience will read on to the second. If the second sentence is interesting, they'll read on to the third – and so on. You can have the call to action as the 100th line, provided the preceding 99 lines were interesting enough for the audience to get that far.

A second reason for seeing less copy is that more and more advertising and marketing has to be 'international'. A TV ad or billboard campaign may run in a number of different countries, all with different languages. It's easier to do that if you don't need to translate the copy for each.

In fact, international advertising makes it nigh-on impossible to do work that involves colloquialisms, wordplay or turns of phrase that are unique to a particular language. Hence work that's more about images than words.

There's a third reason for short copy's prevalence. The widespread belief that people are becoming more and more visual – they read less, they have shorter attention spans, they're too busy.

But people still like to be engaged. People still like what's interesting. And that could still be your copy.

'People read what interests them. Sometimes that's an ad.'

People are busy, and they prioritise, but they're not *too* busy. They might get home and watch three hours of TV. If they're watching commercial TV, in three hours they might see more than 20 minutes of ads.

In summary: copy can be long. As long as it's interesting.

3.14 Avoid a woolly ramble

As Oscar Wilde said, "I'm sorry this letter is so long – I didn't have time to make it shorter."

Long copy is not the same thing as long-winded copy. As we covered in 2.5 of this book, you should always edit. Ruthlessly.

Saying things in twice as many words as needed is the same as being vague. It means your reader can't see the wood for the trees.

Always. Trim. The. Fat.

3.15 Don't get them disagreeing

A simple example is don't describe something as 'unique' when the audience knows it's not. As soon as people start disagreeing with your copy or questioning its credibility, they'll start questioning your product or service's credibility.

Similarly, it's easy to invent a world where everything is astonishing, spectacular, fabulous blah blah blah – I've read plenty of copy that is overblown with superlatives. It just makes the writer sound like a permanently enthralled Disney character, rather than making the product sound any better.

Don't say incredible unless you can prove why, otherwise credibility starts to fall.

In fact, the original meaning of 'incredible' is that it's 'not credible'. Same with 'fantastic' – if something is fantastical then it's not real.

Aim to get your reader on your side and say things they can agree with. Get them nodding along saying 'yes' throughout and you'll make it harder for them to say 'no' when you ask for the sale.

Again, it's what good salesmen do.

They establish rapport, befriend you, agree with you and get you agreeing with them… so they're harder to say no to when they try and flog you something.

3.16 Don't know it, feel it

The difference between rationally knowing something and really feeling it is huge – and an important tenet of persuasive copy.

How many times have you felt a swell of emotion when watching a film? Maybe shed a tear when a character dies… even though you know the whole thing is made up?

So think of what emotions would be most effective in your audience and write your copy to try and create those emotions – whether it's envy or worry or hope or joy or glee or anger: these emotions are likely to be more persuasive than cool, calm logic.

Emotions make something more memorable too. Your own memories – both good and bad – are generally the ones that were of an emotional experience.

3.17 Show not tell

People don't like to be told things as much as they like coming to the conclusion themselves (or thinking they did).

And when they do, it'll be a lot more powerfully believed, because it was their decision.

We just have to nudge them in the right direction.

For example, say you're promoting going to see Irish horse racing. Do you tell people, 'Horse racing in Ireland is very exciting'? Does that make it *seem* exciting?

Or do you say, 'The only sound louder than the thunder of hooves is the pound-pound-pounding of your heart'.

'Telling' is lazy. 'Showing' requires more thought (and sometimes more words) but is a lot more powerful because it engages the audience more deeply.

3.18 Three's the magic number

Writing in threes is a charming, bewitching, seductive writing technique. See?

Lots of things work well grouped in threes – from the Three Wise Men to the Three Musketeers.

And look at any home interiors magazine – you'll see page after page of carefully 'dressed' rooms with a row of three vases, or three items the same colour or three pictures across the same wall.

For some reason, copy works well using threes too. It's a great way to add rhythm, add tone, and reinforce the point you're making.

Look, I just did it again in that sentence – gave three benefits (and before that, I gave three examples – vases, items the same colour, pictures on a wall).

Consider the merits of a few threesomes in your copy.

3.19 Tell them what you want

Obvious, I know. But a lot of copy seems rather shy when it gets to the crunch: asking its reader to do something. It blushes and stutters and ums and ahs around the subject like a teenage boy asking the school hottie on a date.

The 'call to action' is a vital part of any piece of copy. If you're writing to persuade someone to do something… make sure you tell them what it is you want them to do – and be clear about it. If you've seen Glengarry Glen Ross, you'll know the brilliant scene with Alec Baldwin 'motivating' the sales team. "A B C," he says, "Always Be Closing".

No ifs or buts. Literally, no 'ifs'. Don't say, 'So if you want…' as that shows doubt in your copy: it allows for the possibility that they might not want to do what you want them to. Don't entertain that idea – because if your copy shows doubt then the prospect certainly will.

A great set of tube ads by M&C Saatchi London were just copy, no pictures, for dixons.co.uk.

They were printed in the colours and fonts used by different high street stores; so there was one written to look a bit 'John Lewis', about John Lewis. The ad read:

> Step into middle England's best loved department store, stroll through haberdashery to the audio visual department where an awfully well brought up young man will bend over backwards to find the right TV for you
>
> **then go to dixons.co.uk and buy it.**

It was a great, cheeky proposition – 'Use your favourite shops to find the things you like, then save money by buying them online at dixons.co.uk'.

It had a great strapline under the logo too: *Dixons. The last place you want to go.*

Effectively *the whole ad* was a call to action. Never mind copy that sidesteps what it wants you to do, in these great ads *every word* was about what they wanted you to do.

3.20 Urgency

This relates to the previous point 'Tell them what you want'.

Urgency isn't always appropriate – at least, not in the old-fashioned 'Hurry – everything must go' kind of way.

But a sense of *movement* in your copy is nearly always useful.

In a world of bewildering choice, non-stop distractions and information overload, a little direction can be well-received. So don't pussyfoot around too much. Make it clear what you want your reader to do and create some sense of moving towards that action.

You don't have get your reader to run, it's perfectly fine if they walk. Just so long as you get them moving.

The idea behind a 'run' sense of urgency (eg 'Reply now – offer ends soon') is to get your reader to act *while you've still got them persuaded.*

Because the magical power of your copy will wear off over time.

To use Glengarry Glen Ross again, in that film the salesmen are flogging real estate – and there's a cooling off period where customers can cancel. Just as you can with lots of insurance products.

Cooling off periods were introduced because people were being strongly sold to, buying the product then getting second thoughts a few days later, but were unable to back out of the commitment.

You don't want people to back out of the commitment your copy will have elicited from them. So create a sense of urgency to get them to act there and then.

Plus, a genuine feeling of urgency is exciting. It stirs the blood – and that, again, makes for good copy.

Not everything suits this 'hard sell' approach of course. But just bear it in mind, and make sure you are creating a little bit of 'hustle' to get people moving. Even if it's just conveying a sense of 'Now that you know how good X is, why would you wait to enjoy X's benefits?'.

3.21 The tease

Let the reader know that you're going to tell them something interesting…

… in a moment.

Some people don't see the benefit of this approach – indeed, it can seem to contradict what I've said elsewhere, about being simple and leading with what's most interesting to your audience. But a tease *can* work well, providing the copy which comes before 'the main event' is interesting in its own right.

You may be explicit about the tease.

For example

'I'd like to tell you about how you can have the thick, healthy-looking hair you've always wanted. But first, let me ask you what you know about Eskimos.'

You're telling the audience what you're going to tell them 'in a moment'.

However, you can have a more implicit tease.

For example

An ad with the headline 'The thick, healthy-looking hair you've always wanted' then opens with the line 'Let me ask you something. Why is it that Eskimos always have such thick, shiny, healthy hair?'

In that one, there's no 'But first', it just starts with a subject that doesn't seem to be directly related to the headline. But it's intriguing. And because you've promised me a benefit in the headline, I'll read on.

And when it turns out that the Eskimo story is pertinent to how I can have thick, healthy hair (remember, 'relevant abruption') then I'll feel rewarded for persevering. The 'reveal' will actually be more compelling than if you'd just come out with it straightaway.

(I don't know about the Eskimos by the way, I just made that up. Maybe they do have great hair. Probably all that fish full of Omega 3s or something.)

3.22 Make it flow

A piece of copy should flow from the first word to the last.

And all the effort you put into the writing should make it a pleasure to read.

One thing that can interrupt the flow of your copy is an abrupt change of subject. A simple way around it can be to add a few words that link the ideas together. A dab of glue.

These links can be particularly useful when you suddenly have to shoehorn an extra message into your copy, and you need to find an easy way of linking things together without major surgery.

Here are some words and phrases that can link sentences or paragraphs together to keep things flowing smoothly:

What's more,	In fact,
Surprisingly,	Without doubt,
Also,	There's more.
It gets better.	It gets worse.
Not only that,	And
Plus,	However,
Nonetheless,	Nevertheless
One more thing.	So
In addition,	Now
Furthermore,	Which means
But consider	Therefore,

3.23 Paint a picture

You can paint a convincing picture with a lot less than a thousand words.

These 'word pictures' are vital in copy. They create a story in your audience's mind's eye. Gets them to 'picture the scene'.

If you can paint an effective picture – using evocative copy, startling description and emotive language – you will involve the reader more. As soon as they're picturing the scene you've created, they're engaged with what you're saying.

Beginning with 'Imagine…' is a simple trick to help write copy that starts painting a picture. Another way is to make the reader the subject, by writing it all in the second person.

A piece I wrote for homeless charity Shelter began as if the reader (who we wanted to make a donation to their helpline) was someone who was about to become homeless: 'A bitterly cold winter's night. You're hungry. Tired. Terrified. All you own in a bag on your back. And your only hope, a free phone call. But… will we answer?'

4.24 Reframe it

We all have our own way of thinking.

What's obvious to you may be far from clear to me. What I find easy, you may find hard. We're all different, we process information in different ways and we have different experiences to draw upon and use to evaluate what we're presented with.

What you consider to be the best way to explain a product, service, benefit, offer, idea or principle may not be the best way for me to absorb it.

Try 'reframing it'. That is, expressing it in more than one way, through your copy. That way, there's more chance that you'll cover several different 'best ways' for different groups of people.

4.25 Back to the start

Already mentioned in 1.3 of this book under *Interest*, this is a very simple trick where the end refers back to the beginning.

It's like a film that, in the final credits, reminds you some of the best moments of the movie. "Oh yeah," you say, "I loved it when that thing exploded."

You may begin with a creative hook, a surprising line or an interesting idea. Therefore, near the end, refer back to that opening hook.

The Eskimo ad about how to have thick, healthy-looking hair by taking this new supplement, for example. You begin by talking about Eskimos (who have lustrous, healthy hair and who eat lots of fish full of Omega 3). You then move on to how this new supplement is the best way for your body to get Omega 3, which will give you fabulous hair too.

The copy talks more about the supplement, the science behind it, how much it costs and where to buy it… and you haven't mentioned Eskimos since perhaps the second line of your copy.

So now, at the end, refer back to them. Finish by saying how this new supplement is 'The second best way there is to have great hair – the best being to come from Eskimo lineage. Like the current Miss World.'

Breaking the law

And finally that old adage 'When you know the rules, you know when to break them'.

The preceding 25 tips are just that: tips. Not laws. Not objective, unassailable truths. And certainly not exhaustive.

They interact with each other, they depend on the circumstances, the timing, the medium, the audience. That's why great copy is an art, not a science.

Use these tips as a starting point, not a destination. Add new ones. Try new things, new approaches, find new truths. Audiences continue to become more sophisticated. Media continue to fragment. Language continues to evolve.

What makes great copy should continue evolving too – and someone's got to keep raising the bar for what makes copywriting great, and discovering new tips to pass on.

Why not you?

4 The Magnificent Seven:
Copy examples, from brief to execution

4.1 Press ad
The Royal British Legion

4.2 Dimensional mailing
SoundEffects

4.3 Poster
The Alzheimer's Society

4.4 Email
Nando's

4.5 TV
Chelsea Building Society

4.6 Mail pack
NCH

4.7 Blog
My blog

Ok, maybe 'magnificent' is a little vainglorious – since I wrote all the examples here.

But, just as I thought it might be useful to recommend books along the way rather than have a 'recommended reading' list at the end, I thought there might be a better way to do examples.

Most copywriting books are littered with examples of well-known award-winners from around the world over the last 20 years. They fill pages and they look pretty and they can be useful for inspiration.

However, because they weren't actually written by the book's author, they can't really tell you how they were created and what went into them.

Instead, this collection of seven examples – each for a different client, to a different audience, in a different medium – is all stuff written by me. Some won awards. Some got fantastic results. All were well received by the client they were created for (and thank you to the clients here who gave me permission to reproduce the work).

You can see each example much larger (and in glorious Technicolor) at *www.copy-righter.co.uk*.

Here, I've gone over them with a dayglo pen and annotated each one so they've more highlights than a WAG's hair extensions. It means I can show some of the tools explained in the rest of this book in action.

Here's what I did, why and how.

The
Royal
British
Legion

First, two award-winning full page press ads, with QR codes that then take you straight to a mobile-optimised microsite.

The ads are from a series of six for The Royal British Legion – the charity behind Poppy Day (you can see all six at www.copy-righter.co.uk).

I'll go through the copy of one of them in detail, but I wanted to show two here because of how they came about.

You see, The British Legion has two key areas of work. They're the custodians of remembrance – such as when we all come together at 11am on the 11th day of the 11th month to remember those who gave their lives from conflicts long past.

But they're also behind a huge amount of work supporting veterans from current conflicts, returning injured or traumatised.

So we created two variants of the British Legion's tone of voice: *Now* and *Then*. The former for communications that lead with a story about current conflicts, the latter for communications leading with remembrance.

In the *Now* copy (which is in a sans-serif font), the sentences are shorter. More staccato in tone. With the occasional military abbreviation and modern English usage.

By comparison, the *Then* copy (in a serif font) has longer sentences with more traditional English usage. There's occasional language of the time (like 'Tommies') and it's generally bit more reverential and poetic in tone, talking of saluting and honour.

So, the bugle ad is an example of *Then* copy, the other (which I'm going to examine here) is an example of *Now* copy.

As a concept, it's number five from the Book of Brainwaves (in part 2.3): copy led. The art director did a brilliant job of laying the ad out so that the headline could dominate (rather than a more expected approach where you'd have a big picture at the top and the headline going across a single line).

He gave the line impact, and he worked with the rhythm of it. I'd written the headline to balance (lost his legs / find his feet) and the art director used the image to split those two halves of the line. An elegant example, I think, of words and pictures working well together rather than competing with each other.

Lost in the bloody battle of the Somme.

Found in the bric-a-brac of Rotherham.

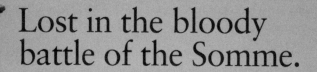

0730 hours. All along the line throats were cleared nervously, hands gripped rifles tight. Then the shrill of whistles pierced the tense silence: the battle of the Somme had begun.

In the trenches of the 8th Battalion York and Lancaster Regiment, a lone bugler sounded the charge. 703 men shinned up ladders and surged forward, their courage tested under the enemy's continual bombardment.

As they ran towards the barbed wire, nine out of ten men fell. Bugler Daniel Clay was one of them and his body was never recovered from the mud of the battlefield.

By the end of that summer's day, thousands had died and the casualty tally stood at over 61,000. It remains the bloodiest day of the British Army's history.

Nine decades later, Maurice Green was rooting around a bric-a-brac stall in Rotherham. He was drawn to a filthy and battered army bugle. He paid £5, took it home and carefully cleaned away the years of grime. And as he polished he saw inscribed on the instrument the service number of his grandfather: Daniel Clay.

Although Private Clay never came home to his family, his bugle did. And once more, on Remembrance Day last year, it sounded the Last Post, summoning up the 'pale battalions' of those brave Tommies who fought for King and country.

Those men who did survive the Great War returned to a changed country. The promise of a land 'fit for heroes' never materialised and it fell to the newly formed British Legion to help brave veterans in need.

Like the bugle, we're still saluting those Service man and woman who have fallen in battle.

11-11-11-11.org.uk

This year is a special anniversary for remembrance. So at 11am on the 11th day of the 11th month of the 11th year, let's remember those who serve and sacrifice. And show them our support.

THE ROYAL BRITISH LEGION

Registered Charity No: 219279

WHEN PETER LOST HIS LEGS

The explosion.

Threw Peter's six tonne, armoured Viking twenty feet.

And when it landed, it took his legs.

That was May 2008. Helmand Province. Lance Corporal Peter Dunning was on patrol, following SOP (Standard Operating Procedure) when he drove over the makeshift mine that changed his life forever.

A double amputation. He spent five months in hospital unable even to turn over in bed. Then: a turning point. A fellow Marine stopped by.

IT TOOK HIM A YEAR TO FIND HIS FEET

"He walked over, wearing his uniform and said: 'I know what you're going through'. I thought, 'That's nice mate, but I've lost both legs!' Then he rolled up his uniform and showed me his prosthetic leg."

Peter spent the next seven months learning to use his own prosthetic legs. And with support from the British Legion he's learned to walk again. He's back in uniform. He's even a member of the Services' disabled ski team.

This year, more and more of our brave boys will be returning from Afghanistan. Wounded. Amputated. Traumatised. They stood up to be counted. Now they're counting on us. On you.

Because unlike Peter, they won't all take their injuries in their stride.

11-11-11-11.org.uk

This year is a special anniversary for remembrance. So at 11am on the 11th day of the 11th month of the 11th year, let's remember those who serve and sacrifice. And show them our support.

THE ROYAL BRITISH
LEGION

Registered Charity No: 219279

When Peter lost his legs it took him a year to find his feet [1]

The explosion. [2]

Threw Peter's six tonne, armoured Viking twenty feet. [3]

And when it landed, it took his legs.

That was May 2008. Helmand Province. Lance Corporal Peter Dunning was on routine patrol, following SOP (Standard Operating Procedure) [4] when he drove over the makeshift mine that changed his life forever.

A double amputation. He spent five months in hospital unable even to turn over in bed. Then: a turning point. A fellow Marine stopped by. [5]

"He walked over, wearing his uniform and said: 'I know what you're going through'. [6]

"I thought, 'That's nice mate, but I've lost both legs!'

"Then he rolled up his uniform and showed me his prosthetic leg."

Peter spent the next seven months learning to use his own prosthetic legs. And with support from the British Legion [7] he's learned to walk again. He's back in uniform. He's even a member of the Services' disabled ski team.

This year, more and more of our brave boys will be returning from Afghanistan.

Wounded. Amputated. Traumatised. [8]

They stood up to be counted. Now they're counting on us. On you. [9]

Because unlike Peter, they won't all take their injuries in their stride. [10]

11-11-11-11.org.uk [11]

Notes

[1] Wax lyrical: This headline, I would suggest, is an example of antithesis, mentioned in 3.7.5.

Peter's story is about how he had his legs blown off. It's the most dramatic, powerful element we have, so we make it the subject of the headline. Then, to turn it into an engaging headline, I looked up phrases and expressions that involve legs, arms, limbs and so on.

For instance, 'Peter's service cost him an arm and a leg. We're not asking you for that much,' maybe. Except that he didn't lose an arm. So, 'finding your feet'. Well, if we can say Peter 'lost his legs' we can compare that with 'find his feet' and we've got a line that goes from problem (his injury) to solution (getting his life back) in a lyrical way that gets attention and engages.

The headline, with the image, is also an example of how you don't 'show and tell'. A headline and image should work together, not simply mimic each other. In other words, don't have a headline that simply describes the image. One should add something to the other.

[2] Be unusual: Not an unusual word in this case – an unusual construction and part of the *Now* tone of voice. I'm sure my English teacher would tell me that 'The explosion' isn't a proper sentence. There's no verb, for one thing. But sometimes breaking the rules of grammar creates a bit of standout and impact.

[3] Be specific: A recurring theme. It's really valuable to imbue your writing with little details that add authenticity and texture to the story. I could have just said 'armoured vehicle'. Instead I found out that it was a six-tonne Viking – making the reader realise just how powerful the explosion was, to throw a six-tonne vehicle 20 feet in the air. Interestingly, spell-check thinks I've got both 'armoured' and 'tonne' wrong – showing you can't always rely on your software.

[4] An example of the military acronyms specific to the *Now* tone of voice variant, giving it a bit of an Andy McNab personality.

[5] Style: The staccato tone is shown clearly in this paragraph. Although the sentences vary in length (which stops it sounding like it's being read by a satnav), in this four sentence para there's a three, four and five word sentence.

[6] Credibility: In 2.4.4 of this book when looking at psychological triggers, I mention how a third party testimonial can add credibility to your own words. Here, it's the voice of the person we're talking about – Peter. By including a direct quote from him, the story is given greater gravitas and authenticity.

[7] Subtlety: Peter is the hero of this story, not the British Legion. Right at the start, in 1.1 of this book, we talked about clarity and focus. Here the focus is on Peter, moving to those like him we need to help. So we don't want to shift focus to being all about the British Legion; it's enough to say they were the organisation which helped him, and by supporting them, you're supporting people like him.

[8] Three's the magic number: Mentioned in 3.18 of this book is the power of three – used here in its most pared down form.

[9] Wax lyrical: It's a copy-led ad that needs to build to a crescendo – a metaphorical call to arms. So we have this bit of wordplay 'stood up to be counted / now they're counting on you'.

[10] Wax lyrical: Structurally, the ad is very simple – from Peter's injury to treatment to recovery, the last section then talking about people other than Peter. So, in the last sentence we make a reference back to him (and the headline), with a play on words; 'stride'. A word with a literal meaning (reminding us that he would find it difficult to stride, as he's lost his legs) and a metaphorical meaning (reminding us of his bravery in dealing with those injuries).

[11] Call to action: There's a discrete panel of copy for the call to action – visiting the microsite we created at 11-11-11-11.org.uk (representing the 11th hour of the 11th day of the 11th month of the 11th year). And next to the url, a QR code to take you straight to a mobile version of the site.

Sound
Effects

This double award winner was for a fairly unpromising product: room insulation, installed by a company called SoundEffects.

There's nothing very interesting to show: it's basically lots of insulating padding between the existing wall and a new wall of acoustic plasterboard. Rival companies tended to show cheesy pictures of people with their hands over their ears and pained expressions on their faces: the 'before'.

The proposition was around the classic 'problem / solution' dynamic: 'Get rid of the unwanted noise disturbance from your neighbours so you can enjoy peace and quiet in your own home.' Our insight was that 'An Englishman's home is his castle'. So, suffering from noise pollution is stressful because it's disturbing you, but also because it feels like you're being attacked in your own 'castle'.

We had two audiences. The doordrop (with a packet of earplugs inside each one) was aimed at homeowners in new-build estates (where the sound insulation between properties isn't always great), as well as flats and terraces in reasonably well-off postcodes.

The other audiences were groups of people: Resident's Associations, Neighbourhood Watch coordinators and other local community groups. They got the more expensive audio mailing examined here.

The concept – well, you could say it came from 'play with the senses' (number 17 of the *Book of Brainwaves* in section 2.3). Or you might say it was 'play with the medium / format' (number 18 from the same section).

Either way, what we wanted to do was recreate the problem as literally as possible.

So, when you open the mailing an audio chip – recorded with terrible, tuneless dance music – starts up. The fact that it's coming from one of those greetings card speakers works well: the sound is distorted just like it would be if it was coming through the wall of next door.

The audio chip in the mailing and the earplugs in the doordrop meant we could bring the idea to life without needing cheesy photography, and gave the copy room to really sell the solution. As you can see:

[front]

Quiet night in? [1]

[reveal, right hand side]

Alas, not tonight... [2]

[letter]

For a little peace and quiet, give us a shout. [3]

Dear homeowner,

Next door's music. [4] Turned up to 11 and pounding through the walls.

Or their bad-tempered Alsatian, barking through the night. Or their five speaker, surround-sound TV. Or the herd of elephants that uses their stairs. [5]

As many as one in three of us [6] suffer from noisy neighbours. It can be incredibly stressful. It can cause sleepless nights and health problems. It can even make you dread going home. [7]

But if you suffer from noisy neighbours and a quiet word hasn't helped, we can.

To block out next door's party, we can soundproof your party [3] wall.

SoundEffects is one of the UK's longest-established, most experienced sound insulation companies [8] – and every year we help many more homeowners reclaim a little peace and quiet. We can do most jobs in two to three days, we'll leave no mess and it's a discreet service so your neighbours will never know. [9]

Most importantly, our sound insulation reduces unwanted noise by as much as 75%. [10]

Our most popular option costs from as little as £825 [9] to sound insulate a wall. We can also insulate floors and ceilings – particularly useful for anyone living in a noisy flat. And after we're done, we'll skim the insulated surface beautifully and re-fix any coving and skirting boards with the minimum of fuss.

Rediscover the wonderful sound of silence. [3] Call SoundEffects on 01234 567890 or visit www.soundeffectslimited.co.uk for a solution that's music to your ears.[3]

Or rather, no music to your ears. [3]

Yours sincerely

Allistair Strudwick

Director of SoundEffects Ltd

P.S. If you don't have a noise problem but know someone who might, please have a quiet word in their ear [3] and pass on our details. Thank you. [11][12]

[underneath letter, on left hand panel]

Fed up with the sound of music? [13]

Call 01234 567890 or visit soundeffectslimited.co.uk for sound insulation that complies with Part E regulations, reduces unwanted noise by as much as 75% and costs from as little as £825 per room.

Compare that to the cost of moving home to escape the noise (on average, around £16,000) [13] and you can see just how much better off you could be by calling SoundEffects today.

Plus: save £50 on soundproofing [14]

Quote AD50 when you get in touch and we'll give you a £50 discount on your sound insulation. £50 you could spend on a takeaway and a nice bottle of wine.

To enjoy a quiet night in.

"At last we have moved back into our sitting room. What a relief to have some peace and quiet!" [8]

– Mr and Mrs Phillips, Cheltenham, Gloucestershire.

Notes

[1] Typographic: Question and Answer. Q and A. It's just a little thing, but the question on the cover begins with a giant Q. And the answer when you open it begins with a giant A.

[2] Write pleasingly: There's a balance between question and answer: both are three words long. Ending this answer with leader dots (or ellipsis as the three dot punctuation mark is known) encourages the reader to read on…

[3] Wax lyrical: This simple bit of wordplay might be *antithesis*, the 4th type of wordplay from 3.7 of this book. 'Peace and quiet' is a common expression, as is 'give us a shout'. Put the two together and you've got a nicely contradictory juxtaposition: you can't literally enjoy quiet if you're shouting.

There are a few more wordplay references to sound throughout the mailing – but not so many that it becomes a game. They're there to maintain the theme and reinforce the story of sound pollution, not show off how many different puns you can come up with.

[4] Start with a short one: The opening sentence is just three words long. The whole paragraph is just 12 words long, making it easy for the reader and drawing them in.

[5] Paint a picture: Instead of just talking about 'it's horrible suffering from noise problems', I've got four different examples (the elephant one being a metaphor, obviously) of how you might be experiencing noise disturbance. That way there's more chance of the reader recognising one of those issues, but it's also a good way of reinforcing the basic theme while saying it in a different way each time so it doesn't sound repetitive.

[6] Just the facts: I found this on the internet (so it must be true). One in three means you needn't feel unusual to need this kind of help. And 'one in three' sounds so much more human than saying '33%'.

[7] Rational and emotional: If noise disturbance is the rational side of the problem, this is the emotional side – how it makes you feel. Very important, to amplify emotions and make the reader feel the problem. Head, heart, hand: engage their head and heart, and you'll get them to use their hand – to contact you and buy your product.

[8] Credibility: We establish that SoundEffects is big and experienced (since you won't have heard of them). A testimonial near the end also adds further credibility – even though you don't know the people giving it.

[9] 'Answer the questions in the customer's mind': Although the letter is fairly short, there's plenty of content; it's not just a load of waffle about how noise is bad. In this paragraph, I'm answering many of the concerns a reader might have, such as whether it's messy, how long it takes, will my neighbours find out and therefore use it as an excuse to be noisier than ever? Oh, and how much does it cost?

[10] Benefit led and specific not generic: Having emphasised the problem, it's important to be clear about the solution. And not by saying 'reduces noise pollution dramatically' or anything vague like that. Here, we're clear: it reduces noise by as much as 75% (see *Quantify*, 3.11 of this book). And note 'as much as' rather than 'up to', as the former sounds bigger.

[11] Second bite at the cherry: There's a clear call to action in the main body of the letter, but there's an alternative in the PS – if you don't suffer from noise, pass this on to someone who might. It's in the PS because sometimes people go to the signatory before they've read the letter, to see who it's from – which means they may take in the PS early on. In which case, people who realise the service isn't relevant for them will know they can pass it on instead.

[12] Structure: Now that we've come to the end of the letter, let's have a look at the structure of it from a simple 'AIDA' (Attention, Interest, Desire, Action) point of view (see the first section in 1.3 of this book, and also the third section of 2.3).

So: it's ten paragraphs long.

The first two identify the customer's problem and dramatise it. (*Attention*)

The third creates the emotional impact of that problem.

The fourth and fifth offer promise of a solution. (*Interest*)

The sixth gives that promise credibility and reassures the audience.

The seventh (in bold) gives the knockout punch: just how good the promise / solution is. (*Desire*)

The eighth, now that we have them hooked, gives the price and covers the mundane aspects.

The ninth gives the call to action, either phone or go online (*Action*).

The tenth has a reprise of the theme, a play on words that also conveys the benefit you're buying.

When you look at it like that, you can see how simple it is – a logical progression that never stands still, never goes back over old ground and never goes off at a tangent.

[13] Comparative mind: The fifth psychological trigger from 2.4 of this book. Here we compare the cost of the soundproofing with the cost of moving home (which is a course of action some people take to escape noisy neighbours). By comparison, the soundproofing is a bargain – about £15,000 cheaper.

[14] Incentive: Always useful to drive response by giving people something extra. Here it's a cash saving, with an example of how you might spend it. Note that it says 'Save £50' rather than '£50 off' since 'save' is one of those hardwired words (3.6 from the *Quick Tips* part of the book). And that we're talking about £50 rather than 5% – people prefer to think about hard cash rather than percentages.

4.3

poster

Alzheimer's
Society

Right: here's an idea that doesn't work in black and white. Sorry about that. However, you can see it in colour at www.copy-righter.co.uk.

It's a crosstrack poster written for The Alzheimer's Society all the way back in 2004, and it's an example of a typographical concept (number 6 from the *Book of Brainwaves* in 2.3 of this book).

The brief was to find a way to make people understand and empathise with what it's like to have Alzheimer's. We also wanted to come up with a fresh, contemporary take on it that didn't need pictures of 'forgetful old people'.

Instead of a conventional headline, it has a list of colours… that are in a different colour to the one they spell.

To see why, see it online and try saying the colour each word *is*, out loud and as fast as you can. Notice that it's actually quite difficult. Then try saying the colour each word *spells*, out loud and as fast as you can – and notice how much faster that is.

There's an explanation of why in the poster, which is over 300 words long. That might seem a lot, but people spend an average of six minutes waiting for the tube. Which means six minutes staring across the tracks at your ad; a great opportunity to draw them in with a word challenge, and more than enough time to read 300 words.

It was shortly after winning the Alzheimer's account that we discovered my mum's father had Alzheimer's disease.

It probably made me think a bit harder about what I was writing. He and his wife had celebrated their Golden Wedding Anniversary (50 years) just a couple of years earlier, yet sometimes in the latter stages he didn't really seem to know her – which was incredibly hard on her.

Anyway, here's the poster, a copywriting award finalist:

Try this mental challenge: out loud and as fast as you can, say the colour each word is (not what it spells):

red green blue orange yellow grey brown purple

Tricky, isn't it? It's almost as if your brain is working against you – because the left side of your brain (the verbal part) is guided by each word's meaning, while the right side (the visual part) is guided by each word's colour.

You can end up more confused than a tourist taking 20 minutes to go from Regent's Park to Great Portland street via the Bakerloo, Victoria and Metropolitan lines... only to emerge blinking in the sunlight and see they've gone just 200 metres.

Now imagine how utterly discombobulating and distressing it would be if your brain was working against you all the time. Playing never-ending, nightmarish mind games with you. A living hell. And a cruel horror faced by 100,000 people a year who develop dementia.

You can be standing in your the street, key in hand... unable to remember which house is yours, even though you've lived there for 20 years. Or, like one person who developed Alzheimer's, you might put the kettle on the hob, but ten minutes later realise it was an electric kettle – which is now burning down the kitchen.

It can be just as distressing for friends and family too. Imagine being sat next to someone on the tube who suddenly, excitedly says they think they recognise you – are you their sister? And having to tell them no. You're their daughter.

There's no cure for Alzheimer's. There is evidence that the occasional glass of red wine may reduce your risk of getting the disease, and we're funding a study into the possible benefits of gingko biloba. There are

also prescribed drugs that can relieve symptoms of the disease, and lots of other ways in which the Alzheimer's Society can help.

So if you think that you or someone you know is becoming increasingly confused, visit our website at alzheimers.org.uk for more information. It's the same website you should visit if you think you're becoming unusually forgetful.

And if you think you're becoming unusually forgetful, visit our website at www.alzheimers.org.uk.

Alzheimer's Society
Dementia care and research
Registered charity no. 296645

Try this mental challenge:[1]

Out loud[2] and as fast as you can, say the colour each word is (not what it spells):

red   green   blue   orange
yellow   grey   brown   purple[3]

Tricky, isn't it? It's almost as if your brain is working against you – because the left side of your brain (the verbal part) is guided by each word's meaning, while the right side (the visual part) is guided by each word's colour.[4]

You can end up more confused than a tourist taking 20 minutes to go from Regent's Park to Great Portland street via the Bakerloo, Victoria and Metropolitan lines… only to emerge blinking in the sunlight and see they've gone just 200 metres.[5]

Now imagine how utterly discombobulating and distressing[6] it would be if your brain was working against you all the time. Playing never-ending, nightmarish mind games with you. A living hell. And a cruel horror[7] faced by 100,000 people a year[8] who develop dementia.

You[9] can be standing in your the street, key in hand… unable to remember which house is yours[9], even though you've lived there for 20 years. Or, like one person who developed Alzheimer's, you might put the kettle on the hob, but ten minutes later realise it was an electric kettle – which is now burning down the kitchen.[10]

It can be just as distressing for friends and family too. Imagine being sat next to someone on the tube [5] who suddenly, excitedly says they think they recognise you – are you their sister? And having to tell them no. You're their daughter.

There's no cure for Alzheimer's.[11] There is evidence that the occasional glass of red wine may reduce your risk of getting the disease, and we're funding a study into the possible benefits of gingko biloba.[4b] There are also prescribed drugs that can relieve symptoms of the disease, and lots of other ways in which the Alzheimer's Society can help.[12]

So if you think that you or someone you know is becoming increasingly confused, visit our website at alzheimers.org.uk for more information. It's the same website you should visit if you think you're becoming unusually forgetful.

And if you think you're becoming unusually forgetful[13], visit our website at www.alzheimers.org.uk.

Notes

[1] A challenge: A simple copy trick, but people often can't resist having the gauntlet thrown down to them in copy. Especially when a) they're standing around with nothing better to do and b) the challenge isn't very taxing and can be done right there and then.

[2] This was an interesting idea: that grumpy Londoners waiting for the tube would try it 'out loud'. Somehow I imagine most of them did it in their head (which still works).

[3] The copy-led concept the whole piece hangs on. For the life of me, I can't remember (no pun intended) where I got the idea from. It may have been from my psychology degree or it may have been from a book of 'optical illusions and other mind benders' I had lying around. Either way, I didn't invent it but I hadn't seen it used in an ad before.

[4] Water cooler moment: We've now explained why this 'mind bender' works – so we've given the audience something they can share with their friends / family / colleagues, to make them seem interesting and clever. So, they've benefited from the poster already – we've given them a kind of answer to 'WIIFM' (What's In It For Me) and they've only got as far as the second sentence.

[4b] More interesting / useful info is near the end: How you might help reduce your risk of Alzheimer's. If the copy has made getting Alzheimer's seem rather dreadful, then the audience will be interested in these little snippets of how to help prevent it – and more likely to go to the website (ie follow the call to action) to find out more.

[5] Context: The ad makes a reference that's relevant to where it's being read. It's in the Underground, so why not make reference to the Underground? Somehow it makes it seem more personal (since that's where the reader is) and more relevant.

Research: As I'm sure you know, because of the way the tube is laid out, not every journey by tube is quicker than walking it above ground. So I just spent some time looking at a map of where tube stations were and comparing it with a tube map – to find a convoluted route that would take longer underground than over. The Londoners who also knew this would nod along, feeling clever (a smile in the mind – one of the psychological triggers in 2.4).

This part of the ad is also an example of using a simile in copy – comparing the feelings of confusion from one thing with the same confused feelings from something else.

A tiny stylistic point is that the sentence is 42 words long – very long, but deliberately so. It's because we're talking about a confusing, convoluted journey, so writing it as one long, meandering sentence is almost onomatopoeic; the sentence reads like the journey would feel.

[6] Be unusual: Mentioned in 3.4 of this book is the idea that the occasional unexpected word can have an interesting effect. It can stop copy from becoming *too* easy to read (ie so easy they're not really taking it in, but skimming it). So: the word *discombobulating*. Here's it's married to simple alliteration by adding *distressing*, which also gives the more uncommon word a clearer meaning.

[7] Emotive language: This is generally quite a 'light hearted' tone for a charity ad, but there are still some strong, emotional words to convey the severity of the condition – here called a 'cruel horror'. We need to get across how bad it is to ramp up the problem which the reader can help solve.

[8] Building the case and specific not generic: After conveying how distressing Alzheimer's is, we add this stat – that 100,000 people a year develop it.

[9] Active style: Here there's plenty of 'you' to make it engaging. Here, 'you' isn't being used in the typical, literal sense, but you as if you were the person with Alzheimer's – another way of 'putting the reader in their shoes'.

[10] 'Product interrogation': This story of someone putting an electric kettle on the hob is true and brings the story to life. These bit of detail, these 'nuggets' are really important to find.

[11] Building the case part 2: From describing Alzheimer's to the stat about 100,000 new cases a year; we now we hit them with the really bad news – if you get it, there's no cure. A short, five word sentence gives it extra impact and establishes the need. So, while talking about Alzheimer's in an interesting way, we've (almost incidentally, it seems) managed to ratchet up a feeling of self-interest: 'Getting Alzheimer's sounds bad… and 100,000 a year get it… and there's no cure.'

We've got the audience (on a small and sub-conscious level) a bit worried for themselves – again, making them more likely to visit the website. It's another way we're moving towards the call to action and creating a subtle sense of urgency.

[12] Problem / solution: Here we offer the solution – contacting The Alzheimer's Society for help. It's important to have 'need' but it's important to have 'solution' too – the sunshine after the rain, if you like.

[13] Diacope: Wax lyrical example 6 (repeating a phrase) from 3.7 of this book. Okay, perhaps repeating the 'forgetful' line was an obvious trick, but it's not meant to be flippant, just a final nod to demonstrating what it can be like to have Alzheimer's.

Here's an email for Nando's, a really cheerful and enthusiastic brand to work on.

The email's not big and it's not clever. But that's kind of the point with this medium.

Get in, hit the reader with a clear, simple benefit, some genuine news – and get out.

So there's no concept, no great psychology and no subtle wordplay (just a few sledgehammer puns).

But it is an example of paying careful attention to the *Context Pyramid* of brand, audience and medium.

Firstly, brand. It's a fun, passionate brand with a Portuguese flavour – and that needs to come across in the copy. They use lots of fun puns in their restaurants, menus and on the website, so we've got a few here. But they never use language which 'insults' the chicken. No wordplay which talks about chicken as an animal, rather than food.

Secondly, audience. The main audiences are families and young adults, so the copy has to appeal to both groups. It can't be too family-focused, but neither can it be edgy. And to help share the excitement with the audience, there are a number of exclamation marks (the other six *Examples* of copy have only two other exclamation marks between them, and both of those are quotes).

And thirdly, medium. You've got short copy. Short sentences. Simple ideas.

It also follows a fair bit of basic email 'best practice'; such as having the same navigation menu as appears on the website. Click-throughs in the main copy. Copy in normal text not as an image (so it'll appear even if the email viewer has images turned off). We've also made sure that the subject line isn't going to get spammed.

The only real trick we've missed is that we haven't got an attention-grabbing benefit 'above the fold' (ie visible in an email preview pane) – because that isn't the Nando's house style.

An email is usually seen on screen of course, so you can see it online at www.copy-righter.co.uk.

Oh oh! It's not working. **Click here** to view online.

 March 2011

Menu | Experience | Careers | Shop & Recipes | Contact us | **Search for your Nando's**

Hi #[Person/salutation]#!
Make no bones about it – our new flame-grilled butterfly chicken is utterly delicious!!

Two succulent chicken breasts with PERi-PERi spice, crispy skin and no bones, it's flame-grilled and fabulous. Add chips or a salad and that's one mouth-watering dish not to be missed.

It's just become available at your local Nando's. So catch our butterfly chicken while it's hot. Or medium, or lemon and herb – however you like it!

new
Flame-grilled butterfly chicken breast

April 3 — Treat Mum, Portuguese style!

This Mother's Day, why not treat mum to dinner at Nando's, or maybe our Nandos Gift Card would make the perfect Mother's Day card! You just take care of mum – and we'll take care of the washing up!

Our new menus look good enough to eat
(though that might spoil your appetite)

Here at Nando's we appreciate fine art as much as we love chicken. That's why our new menus copy the styles of some of the world's greats. Including Warhol, Lichtenstein, Kandinsky and many more. Can you guess which is which?

We're especially passionate about commissioning original work from South African artists (where the PERi-PERi is from). And we've got one of the biggest collections in the world, which you'll find on the walls of all our restaurants for you to enjoy.

And the winner is...

Congratulations to Selina, who was shell-shocked to discover she'd won our recent 'Pop to Cork' competition.

Soon she'll be jetting off to enjoy the craic (and the chicken) in Cork, where we recently opened our fifth restaurant in Ireland.

Good things come in threes
– like our **NEW** Nando's restaurants!
Click the links to find out more.

Manchester Fort	Carlisle	Blackpool
Opened	Opened	Opened
16th Feb	24th Feb	2nd March

Follow Us

Subject: Try our beautiful new butterfly chicken, [Name]! [1]

HOT NEWS FROM NANDO'S

Uh-oh – it's not working. *Click here* to view it online.[2]

[image]

NEW[3] Flame-grilled butterfly chicken breast

Hi [Name][2]

Make no bones about it[4] – our new *flame-grilled butterfly chicken* is utterly delicious![5]

Two succulent chicken breasts with PERi-PERi spice, crispy skin and no bones, it's flame-grilled and fabulous.[6] And it's just become available at your local Nando's.[7]

So *catch our butterfly[8] chicken* while it's hot. Or medium, or mild[9] – however you like it!

[mother's day]

Treat mum, Portuguese style!

This Mother's Day, why not treat mum to dinner at Nando's. Or maybe our Nando's *gift card* would make the perfect Mother's Day card? So you can take care of mum – and we'll take care of the washing up![10]

[menu designs]

Our new[3] menus look good enough to eat (Though that might spoil your appetite)

Here at Nando's we appreciate fine art almost as much as fine chicken. That's why our new menus pay tribute to some of the greats, including Warhol, Kandinsky, Matisse and Lichtenstein. Can you guess which is which? [11]

We also commission original work from South African artists (where the PERi-PERi is from). In fact, we've got *one of the biggest collections* in the world [12] – which you can see on the walls of all our restaurants.

[competition winner]

And the winner is...

Congratulations to Selina, who won our recent 'Pop to Cork' competition. Soon she'll be jetting off to enjoy the craic (and the chicken) in Cork, where we recently opened our fifth restaurant in Ireland!

[new stores]

Good things come in threes – like our new[3] Nando's restaurants!

Click here now!

Manchester Fort Opened 16th February

Carlisle Opened 24th February

Blackpool Opened 2nd March

Notes

[1] Subject line attention: We're careful not to use words that will get the email spammed, but which still convey some news and benefit. Using the person's name in the subject line helps too.

[2] Brand: The standard bits of email copy – about not being able to view it in your browser or wanting to unsubscribe – could have stayed standard. But instead, we've maintained some attention to detail and changed them to fit the Nando's tone of voice. Even the opening 'Hi Name' rather than 'Dear Name' is done to suit the friendly personality of the brand.

[3] Theme: The email doesn't really have a concept, but it does have a bit of a theme: newness. This email doesn't have an offer, it's just 'keeping in touch', but it does manage to feel like it's conveying some real 'news' by talking about new restaurants, new menu designs and the new menu item.

It's much better to have an email that has some kind of theme to it (and notice how visually, the butterflies appear in different parts of the email) rather than just feel like a random collection of subjects being thrown at you.

Of course, 'new' is also one of those hardwired words, mentioned in 3.6 of this book.

[4] Rationale benefit: This is one of the client's lines – to let you know that butterfly chicken doesn't have any bones, unlike most Nando's chicken dishes.

[5] Emotional benefit: The rest of the line is also about how great this new menu item is. This is a useful approach in emails: talk about the main benefit straight away, as upfront as you can so there's no chance of missing it.

[6] Build the case: This is like when I talked about propositions and *The Sun* in Part 2 – looking at how their subhead builds on the headline, and the first sentence builds on the subhead. Here, the second sentence builds on the first, giving more detail to the benefits of this new product.

[7] Call to action: Implicit rather than explicit here; by suggesting it's 'just become available' you're using a little psychology to drive people to a restaurant – people love to be the first to see something / know about something / try something.

[8] Wax lyrical: This gentle play on words, 'catch our butterfly' is the kind of thing you'll see on all sorts of Nando's communications.

[9] Wax lyrical: And here's another gentle example – the double meaning of hot, which also lets us remind customers that you can have Nando's chicken with either hot, medium or mild PERi-PERi spice.

This fifth sentence is also the last of the main story, demonstrating how quick and pithy you should be in emails.

[10] Product interrogation: Back in Part 2 we looked at interrogating all the benefits of a Banana Guard. Here, it's looking at what all the benefits of taking mum to Nando's on Mother's Day might be. How about as well as it being nice for her, there's a benefit for you: it's easy. You won't even have to do any washing up.

[11] Involvement: I've frequently mentioned the idea of using your copy to involve the audience. Here, it's very simple: work out which menu is which style. And when they do it and achieve it, they'll feel good (2.4.12 in this book: a smile in the mind).

[12] Water cooler moment: It's nice to be able to tell the audience that Nando's buys lots of real South African art; it helps convey authenticity of their passion for their heritage.

Chelsea Building Society

I ummed and ahhed over which TV ad to include. In the end, I've chosen one of the simplest and most inexpensive I've ever been involved with. A 60 second DRTV ad for the Chelsea Building Society.

I've worked on TV ads that had a lot more copy and ones where the copy was cleverer and required greater skill to craft.

But I still like the simplicity of this ad (watch it at www.copy-righter.co.uk). For a DRTV ad, where you're pushing for someone to act right there and then (by phoning the number onscreen), it's got quite a low word count. When you present, you might expect to talk at a rate of 100 words a minute. This ad has only 89 words in a minute. Simple, stripped-back, to the point, benefit led. Flourish free.

The ad is set in just one location. There are only two actors. And there's no dialogue. All of which help keep the cost down.

The product is a mortgage that gives you 6% of the mortgage you take out as cash. Kind of like equity release.

The audience are the people in the ad – young homeowners and families.

The concept is very simple: a couple are vying on how to spend their 'cash lump sum'. They communicate their ideas using the fridge door – pictures torn out of magazines and fridge magnets. It means we're able to show a number of different things that the audience might want to buy with their money.

Then, just to give it a bit of levity, there's a twist at the end: the woman is pregnant, which she lets the man know about using the fridge door, showing him that actually they're going to be spending the money on baby stuff.

But read the male voiceover (MVO) and you can see how it almost works like a radio ad.

Although the pictures do add to the story, the voiceover does all the explaining and is complete without the pictures. Since the audience may be making a cup of tea, in earshot of the TV but not watching it.

= £5,100 cash on a
mortgage of £85,000

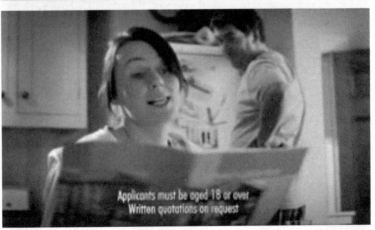

Applicants must be aged 18 or over
Written quotations on request

0800 341 341

In a couple's kitchen. The man walks into shot, puts down his coffee and puts a Chelsea cashback mortgage press ad on the fridge using magnets. He then starts writing something with the magnet letters.

MVO: A Chelsea cashback mortgage is the easy way to get your hands on a substantial cash lump sum. [1]

Time has passed. The woman walks in, carrying shopping bags. She puts them down and looks at what is on the fridge. We see that the man has written PAY OFF CREDIT CARDS. She pushes these to one side, and starts writing something of her own.

Supers: **6% of your mortgage back**

MVO: Several thousand pounds. [2] To spend whenever you wish. On whatever you want. [3]

Supers: **= £5,100 cash on a mortgage of £85,000**

Time has passed. The man comes to the fridge and looks at it before opening the door. Opening it brings the words written on it in front of the camera, so we can read NEW BATHROOM.

MVO: You don't have to move home. And there are no arrangement fees. [4]

Time has passed and we can tell it's night. The woman comes down the stairs in her pyjamas and takes a jar of pickles from the fridge. She closes the door, sees that he's put up a beach picture with the magnets reading BIG HOLIDAY and she deliberately messes them up by rubbing her back against them.

MVO: It's easy too – everything can be arranged by phone and post. [5]

The next morning. The woman is sat at the table. The man comes in and sees that she's made a big arrow out of the magnets, pointing to a picture of a conservatory. He looks at her and she turns, revealing that she's flicking through a brochure of conservatories.

MVO: To find out more – including whether you could save money on your repayments [6] – call free on 0800 341 341. [7]

> *Time has passed. The woman is putting a large cake into the fridge. Closing the door reveals that the man has torn an ad selling a sports car out of the paper and stuck it on the fridge.*
>
> *Next scene. The man goes to the fridge and takes out a beer. He closes the fridge door and looks at it. We can't see what's on it – but we can see his stunned expression, and as he opens his beer, it sprays on him.*

MVO: The Chelsea cashback mortgage. [8]

> Supers: [graphics screen] [logo] **0800 341 341**

MVO: Of course, you might already know how you'll spend your cash lump sum. [9]

> *Cut back to scene: now we see that on the fridge, the woman has written DAD in fridge magnets and put up a picture of a baby and a nursery. The camera cuts to show the woman walk in, smiling. They put their arms around each other as he takes in the news – she's pregnant.*

Notes

[1] Benefit led: A very simple opening. The very first words say what the product is, followed by what it gives you (big lump of cash) with an additional, qualifying benefit (it's easy).

[2] Be specific: What's substantial? Several thousand pounds. In fact, the supers on screen at the time tell you that it's 6% of the mortgage, giving an example of how much that could mean.

[3] Build the benefits: More good news, moving us from 'Interest' to 'Desire'. And note how short the sentences are – you don't want your voiceover to be tripping over long, convoluted phrases.

[4] Q&A: It's important to answer any questions the customer might have which could stop them from responding. So, if research tells us people think, 'Sounds great, but I bet half of it goes on arrangement fees' we must tell everyone 'No arrangement fees'.

[5] Build the benefits part 2: Just keep giving the customer reasons to respond.

[6] Build the benefits part 3: A secondary benefit to the cashback is that you might even lower your monthly repayments – this just gets better and better. But it's not the lead benefit, so we don't try and weave it into the opening, we fire our big guns first, then when the smoke's cleared, fire our next biggest.

[7] Call to action: It's only said once, which is perhaps a mistake, but it does appear on screen four times in 60 seconds.

[8] Name check: People often remember a TV ad... but forget who it's for. There are only 89 words in this ad, but 'Chelsea cashback mortgage' is said at the beginning and end of the ad, as well as a 'graphics screen' with the Chelsea logo and product name on.

[9] Sell the dream: Quite nicely, we leave people with a (subtle) invitation to imagine how they'd enjoy spending 'several thousand pounds'.

Here's an example of long copy: the 700 word letter for a fundraising direct mail pack.

It was created for NCH back in mid 2008, before they became Action for Children (and this pack no longer fits with their current brand).

The brief was to create a mailing that would get as many supporters as possible to make a donation to NCH's work after reading how they'd helped a girl called Emily.

Emily's story was a really traumatic one – she'd been physically and emotionally abused by her mum, for years. From the *Book Of Brainwaves* (in 2.3 of this book) we used concept technique number nine: *storytelling*. We thought it might be powerful to make the whole pack look, feel and read like a child's illustrated 'scary storybook'; the kind you might find in W H Smiths.

The twist was that the little girl in the story wasn't frightened of monsters under the bed or creatures in the cupboard. It was her own mum who terrified her. So we did dark, child's-horror-story-style illustrations. The letter began 'Once upon a time'. Because the letter folded like a book, we had a real pop-up when you opened it. And a bookmark in the mailing, as a gift for their donation.

And throughout, the concept and copy were crafted to suit BAM – Brand, Audience and Medium.

The work was an award finalist for copywriting and beat its ambitious targets for response and income by more than 40%.

Here's the copy and 20 of the things that went into it:

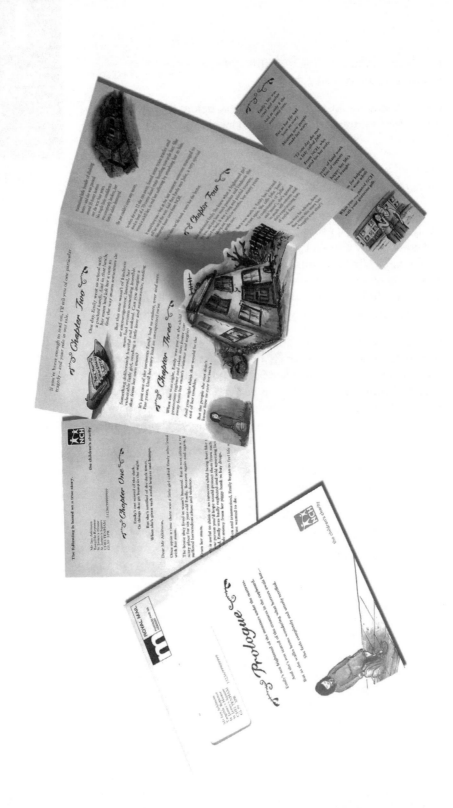

[envelope]

– Prologue – [1]

Emily's not frightened of the monsters under the mattress.

And she's not scared of the creatures in the cupboard.

But as she walks home, wondering what horrors await her...

She feels completely and utterly terrified.[2]

[letter]

A true story.[3]

– Chapter One – [1]

Emily's not scared of the dark.

Or things that go bump in the night.

But she's terrified of the dark times.

When mum gives her such bruises and bumps.

Dear Mr Sample

Once upon a time[1], there was a little girl called Emily who lived with her mum in a very scary house.[4]

It wasn't haunted. But Emily was still very frightened of going home. Because again and again, when she was at home, Emily suffered terrible abuse and violence.

From her mum.[5]

Isn't it awful, to think of an innocent child being hurt like that by the one person you'd[6] hope would protect them from such cruelty?[7] Instead, Emily was badly neglected and told upsetting lies. Mum even stole money from her piggy bank to buy drugs.[8]

Heartbroken and traumatised, Emily began to feel life wasn't worth living. She just wanted to die.[9]

If you're brave enough to read on, I'll tell you of one particular tragedy – and your role in our tale.[10]

– Chapter Two – [11]

One day, Emily went to school with a packed lunch. And in that lunch, her mum had left her a note to find, the way mums sometimes do.

But this note wasn't of kindness or encouragement. Instead, her mum had written something horrible. Something deliberately hurtful and unkind.[8] Can you imagine a vulnerable little girl, needing a little love and reassurance, reading that from her own mum?[7]

It's just one of the torments Emily had to endure, over and over. For years. Until her story had an unexpected twist.

– Chapter Three –

When she was eight, Emily was put on the child protection register and taken into foster care, away from her mum's violence and neglect.[12]

And you might think that would be the end of her troubles.

But the people she met didn't know how to care for such a traumatised little bundle of shaking bones[13] – and she was passed around 30 foster homes over the next four years. Her fragile little confidence was completely broken, her faith in adults destroyed.

She just couldn't cope anymore.

So, when she was 12 she ran away, found some train tracks and stood in front of a 70-tonne diesel train[14] hurtling towards her. She wanted it to kill her, to end her suffering by smashing her to bits.

It would have too – but at the last moment someone managed to pull her out of the way. And then Emily met Julie, a very special therapeutic foster carer from NCH.

And that's when Emily's life took a turn for the better.

– Chapter Four –

Julie understood Emily. She knew what a frightened girl she was, and just how much patience and kindness she needed to heal from all the pain and cruelty she'd suffered.

It was a long, difficult journey, taking not weeks or months, but many years of gentle care. But it was worth it. Emily has learned to trust again. She calls Julie 'Jum' (a combination of 'Julie' and 'mum')[8], she's gained so much self-esteem and she's experiencing lots of joyful days.

You may be asking, does that mean this story has a 'happily ever after'?[1]

Well, yes and no. Emily is 17 now. Her life is full of plans for the future and she's hoping to live independently soon.[15]

But there are other children just like her. Some of them have been through experiences even more distressing – horror stories[1] I can't bear to describe.

They need our help right now[16], and that's where a really important character joins our story.

You.[17]

Please, make a donation today[16] of whatever you can afford, to help our work. With your support, we'll be able to reach another Emily. Another terrified child. We can help them start to heal. And show them life is worth living.[18]

Please, be one of the heroes of our story.[19] Your donation is needed so urgently[16] – and it could help transform the life of another little girl or boy. As a small token of our thanks, we've included a simple bookmark for you.[19]

And thank you for reading Emily's tale.[20] We've reached the end of this story.[1] But your gift will mean a new beginning for a desperate child who feels they have no-one to turn to.

Please, reply as soon as you can.[16]

Yours sincerely,

Name Surname

Job title

Notes

[1] Concept: The copy matches the concept. The content, format and illustrations are themed around a storybook, so the copy is too. It begins with a 'Prologue' on the outer, to a 'Once upon a time' opening to the letter, followed by 'Chapter...' subheads throughout, a 'happily ever after' just before the call to action and the 'we've reached the end of our story' mention right near the end.

[2] Be emotional: I've spoken a lot about the importance of emotion in copy – and sometimes, talking about emotions can help engender them. Here, the idea of a little girl's powerful emotion – fear – is reinforced with rhythmic repetition: 'frightened, scared, terrified'.

This copy on the outer envelope is also a bit unexpected: envelopes usually have a short line of copy, not a whole paragraph. This gives it a little stand out. It also has intrigue – you want to open it to discover what 'horrors' await her.

[3] Credibility: although this is done in the style of a fictional story, we want to assert early on that Emily isn't made up: she's real and what we're describing really happened to her.

[4] To make it easy to read and draw you in, a short opening paragraph: just a single sentence.

[5] The payoff to the preceding paragraph, this one is just three words long. It could have just been tagged on to the end of the previous sentence, but having these three little words by themselves gives them great prominence and impact.

[6] Active style: The first mention of 'you', which then appears regularly throughout the letter, keeping the copy involving.

[7] A rhetorical question you can't help but agree with: by having the reader nod along saying yes, they're being more involved, more in agreement with you and therefore more likely to do what you later ask (make a donation).

[8] Be specific: Here, an example of Emily's mum's cruelty. Getting these bits of detail was really important to illustrate the theme and add authenticity.

[9] Here, we're being as strong as possible, as emotive as possible. The client could have balked at talking about a child wanting to die, but it's what she said, so we were able to use it and really bring home how desperate the situation was.

[10] The tease: We hint at what we're going to tell the reader, if they keep on reading. But we do it as a challenge – 'if you're brave enough'. Of course the reader will think they're brave enough, and will read on just to prove it.

[11] In long copy, subheads can break up long passages of text to make it look easier to read. In truth, I don't tend to use subheads in mailings that often because it makes a letter seem less personal. But that wasn't an issue here, since the whole letter is designed like part of a child's scary story, so subheads were useful. Having them as 'Chapter 2, Chapter 3' etc also helped move the story along.

[12] The story has a pace to it: although the letter is more than 700 words long, it never stands still or repeats itself. It's always going forward in time and intent.

[13] Wax lyrical (3.7 in the *Quick Tips* section): It can be just a phrase or description that adds impact – here describing Emily as 'a traumatised little bundle of shaking bones'. There aren't many bits of waxing like that in the copy though – more than one or two makes you sound like a frustrated novelist.

[14] Be specific: This is a different example of detail which brings a story to life, compared to [8]. In this case, I knew it was a train that Emily had stepped in front of, I just looked it up on the internet to find that UK trains are diesel-powered and weigh 80 tonnes.

[15] 'Solutions not problems' (3.8 in the *Quick Tips* section of the book) isn't quite so relevant in fundraising copy – you need to talk about both, not just the solution. All the way through the copy it's all about the need, the problem – until here, where we turn to the solution.

[16] Urgency: Here we do it literally by asking people to respond 'today', 'urgently' and 'as soon as you possibly can'.

[17] Active style: There's lots of 'you' throughout the letter and here, the most important use of 'you' in the whole letter (and a bit of flattery calling 'you' the most important character in the story).

[18] 'Emotional decisions' (the 10th psychological trigger in section 2.4 of the book) is used here. Step back from the story and you'll notice that although we're asking for a donation and saying that it will help 'transform' a child's life, we don't go into detail as to *how*.

There's very little rational argument about what, precisely, will be done with your money. Instead, we move them emotionally and drive them to respond while they're in this heightened state of emotion.

[19] WIIFM. What's in it for the reader? Well, we're not selling a product or service, we're asking for a donation. But we can make them feel good about donating – here, a donation will make them 'one of the heroes of our story'. And, we can give them a free bookmark – *mutuality* (the 8th psychological trigger from 2.4 of this book). We've given them something, so they feel more compelled to give something back.

[20] There are several references near the end of the letter which link neatly back to the theme at the beginning, so the whole piece feels consistent and complete.

No picture this time, since it's a text-only blog – an example of owned media (see 'digital' in the *Medium* section of 2.2 of this book). It appeared on four different websites and I also tweeted a short url link to it on Twitter and LinkedIn.

My blog

At the start of this book we looked at *specific objective*. What's the objective of a blog?

Well, if you're doing a company blog, hosting it on your website means the homepage is changing regularly, helping it rise up search rankings. Especially if your blog is also chock full of keywords.

If you talk about an interesting subject in a lucid / cerebral / gossipy / insightful / controversial way, you'll also encourage debate and actively drive traffic to the site as people want to hear your thoughts. That's also true if you write a blog that's genuinely useful, providing tips or ideas or advice.

Also, a blog is often your chance to cut free a little. If you read the blog piece below, you'll find its 'voice' is very similar to the tone of the rest of this book. It's just me, writing the way that suits me, without trying to shape the tone to suit any particular brand or audience.

It's not a masterclass in blog writing: far from it. The headline, for example, is not intriguing or promising or even relevant. And it's not going to be picked up on a keyword search.

But I wrote it that way because sometimes it's nice to have a break from doing everything properly, and just write the way that feels good. Quickly, loosely and noisily.

Bloody students [1]

"I don't like any of your ideas," I told a roomful of advertising students on Monday.[2]

"And I certainly wouldn't show any of them to a client."

Oh yes, I'm a tough macho no-nonsense badass who tells it like it is.[3]

Didn't manage to make any of them cry though. Just sulk. Which, since they were teenagers, was hardly much of an achievement.[4]

Let me explain: agency founder Nick Thomas and I, in our role as creative gurus, help out with the local university's advertising degree.

And we'd given the new batch of students a charity brief to crack – a live brief we're working on for an integrated campaign across TV, press and online.

It was a tough brief, in truth. And the students had made a good attempt at it, with some interesting, imaginative stuff that was nicely integrated, neatly scamped and very confidently presented (though often really badly spelled).

But I didn't think any of their ideas were right because they'd all gone down the route of 'borrowed interest'.[5]

Which means that instead of work featuring human beings, I got storyboards featuring squirrels. Rugby players. Magic bottles of cure-all medicine. Coin-operated satnavs. Flocks of birds in synchronised flight. And Monopoly.[6]

Not one of them had portrayed the world, the company or the people as they really were.

Borrowed interest can work well, of course. When your audience has no idea what your product or service is, an analogy can be a useful way to show them 'Our X which you don't know is like this Y which you do know'.[7]

But clumsily done (as it so often is), borrowed interest suggests that 'We couldn't find anything interesting to say about our own product / service, so we thought we'd show you this instead.'[7]

For an example of borrowed interest in action, there's the new Kronenbourg TV ad.[8]

They've got ol' Lemmy Motorhead at the bar singing *The Ace of Spades* in a slow, ballady re-imagining. With the endline 'Slow the pace'.

Seems more like a concept for Guinness to me (since they've made a virtue of the slowness it takes to pour their pint). Maybe Guinness turned the idea down, so the agency sold it to Kronenbourg instead.[9]

Also seems like a strange shift in positioning for French fizzy lager. Are the French known for 'slowing the pace'? Apart from when they're on strike, obviously?[10]

Regardless of whether or not it's good brand positioning, this kind of borrowed interest seems to work ok for a lager. There's only so much you can go on about its ingredients after all. And very little else you can say, what with the alcohol advertising rules being what they are.

But generally, if someone shows you a concept that's based on borrowed interest, ask yourself if that's really the best way to bring the proposition to life. Or if actually, we should just dig a bit deeper and find what's compelling in your actual product / service.[7]

Anyway, students: not all of them are sulky of course. In fact, we've just taken on a graduate team from the university as trainee copywriter and art director. I'll be giving them the 'borrowed interest' sermon on their first day.

In my macho badass way, obviously.

Notes

[1] As I said in the introduction to this piece, this is not a good headline. No keywords, no '10 ways to' promise, no 'Why I'm (something sensationalist)' approaches.

The only defence I can make is that it's not a blog that's trying to accrue as many subscribers as possible (who would then only be disappointed by its infrequent updates). It's more about saying something interesting once in a while that gives an insight into agency life and which means our website homepages have something new appear on them.

[2] Instant action: This is better; an opening that refers to something that's just happened – something with a bit of tension. The idea that there's a roomful of people who I'm 'confronting' in some small way is intriguing.

[3] Christ, I cringe to read that now. Yes I was being ironic, but very poorly. You often find people trying to be amusing in their blogs but failing badly. Like here.

[4] Another attempt at humour. Sorry.

[5] The reveal: this is the real topic of the piece – an opinion piece on the merits (or not) of 'borrowed interest' as a conceptual approach. Lots of blogs use this structural conceit: using a recent, real experience of the author as a 'way in' to explore a bigger theme.

[6] Exemplum: A good sample of the borrowed interest devices the students came up with. Examples always explain your point better than just the theory.

[7] Definition: Three paragraphs that explain what borrowed interest is, when it can be useful, and when it can't be. If you're going to explain something over a long piece (and this blog entry is more than 500 words long), it's still wise to have a 'capsule summary' that explains the main point very succinctly.

[8] Topical and multimedia: I'm referring to a well-known ad at the time. Now we've got owned media (the blog) talking about bought media (a TV ad). In fact, Kronenbourg turned the ad into an integrated campaign (including social media). The focus became not the ad but the song that had been specially recorded for it. People talked about it online, Kronenbourg advertised its existence ad infinitum on Spotify and you could download the track from the Kronenbourg website.

[9] Insight: This is probably the only moment of actual thinking in the blog – where I point out that the positioning of the ad might have been more suited to Guinness than Kronenbourg. A moment of thought-provocation is really valuable in a blog – too many blogs are simply people deriding stuff they've seen around them.

[10] Topical: At the time, many French unions had been striking about the government's austerity measures. Topicality, of which there are several occurrences here, are important in blogs. People don't want to feel like they're reading an article that may have been lying around for years. They want it to be personal (so they can be personal in their reply) and of the moment, so it feels current and relevant to them.

5 Appendices

5.1 How to brief

5.2 How to give feedback

5.3 How to deal with amends

5.4 How to get better

The appendix has no known function in humans.

Here? Well, you be the judge. Four mini-diversions: the first two for people who brief copywriting, the last two for people who do copywriting.

5.1

How to brief

Seen the ceiling of the Sistine Chapel?

It's not bad, is it?

Now, when Pope Julius II briefed Michelangelo to paint it, what do you think he said?

1. "Please paint the ceiling."

   Probably not. He might have got a nice all-over magnolia.

2. "Please paint the ceiling using red and green paint. Oh, and some of that lovely orange."

   It's unlikely. Not only does it not tell Michelangelo what to paint, it gives him a number of restrictions without rhyme or reason.

3. "We've got damp. And cracks. Could you paint over them?"

   The brief still doesn't give him much direction. And it gives irrelevant and depressing information which suggests no-one is interested in what he paints because the ceiling is buggered anyway. How much effort is he likely to put in?

4. "Please paint biblical scenes which should include some / all of the following: God, angels, cupids, devils and a couple of saints."

   Better, perhaps: at least the Pope's beginning to give Michelangelo a steer. It contains the basics, but it doesn't go that extra step, towards a solution. And it's not a very rousing brief.

Here's what Pope Julius II (apparently) said to Michelangelo:

"Please paint our ceiling for the greater glory of God and as an inspiration and lesson to his people.

"Frescoes which depict the creation of the world, the Fall, mankind's degradation by sin, the divine wrath of the deluge and the preservation of Noah and his family."

Of course, the brief lacked a deadline and the ceiling took four years… but hey, look at it.

And the story illustrates a simple point: briefs should inspire, not constrain.

They should have a single-minded proposition. They should be tight and specific, not vague and woolly. And they should contain an insight into the audience.

'Give me the freedom of a tight brief,' goes the saying.

In other words, "Please paint the ceiling" is just too vague. It means the artist has to do everything – come up with not just the concept and the execution of that concept, but also the very subject and positioning and understanding of the audience. With no notion of whether or not you're going to be happy with what they do.

So, buy yourself a Pope hat from a fancy dress shop and write a brief with lashings of inspiration. Or paint your face blue and deliver your brief like the speech from *Braveheart*, where Mel Gibson rouses his troops before battle.

And finally, remember that a brief should give the person / people you're briefing as much help as possible. If a brief is about cracking a puzzle, it's also about providing everything we know so far on how to crack that puzzle.

Write a brief in a way that means everyone is buzzing with ideas at the end of the briefing. Not scratching their heads thinking 'What the hell was that all about?'

Giving feedback is a weighty responsibility.

Reading this book should help tell you what to look for in the copy you're reviewing. Then it's just a matter of deciding how you're going to go through your thoughts with the writer.

That's my first tip, by the way, that they're 'thoughts', not 'amends'.

Telling a copywriter you've got amends suggests you have some changes which need to be made, full stop. No discussion. Which may get your writer's back up. Amends are a monologue. Thoughts are a dialogue.

Here are six things to think about.

1. Be kind.

You might think creative types are indulged, self-indulgent, precious little ego-trippers who swan about in a fantasy world and wouldn't know a tough day at the office if it hit them over the head with an in-tray.

And of course you're absolutely right.

But on the other hand, copywriting means having to put up with 'personal' criticism of your work. Which can be very wearing.

So be kind in the way you comment. And remember: it's easier to destroy than create.

Start your feedback by playing 'Angel's advocate'. The opposite of devil's advocate, instead of looking for what's wrong, look for what's right. Be vocal about everything that's good.

Apparently, when Gordon Brown was Prime Minister, ministers gave him a 'Shit sandwich'. Good news first, then the bad news in the middle, then a bit of good news to finish. It was supposed to make the bad news (of which there was always plenty) more palatable.

Great copy is delicate and often so are its creators. You'll do a lot better to work with them collaboratively rather than confrontationally.

So be gentle. And start with the big picture, not a small detail. It doesn't do you any favours if your first comment is about an apostrophe rather than the concept or tone or overall strength of the copy.

2. Be mean.

While your style should be kind, thoughtful, positive and involve chocolate muffins, your substance should be genuine, honest and challenging. Not feedback to water work down, to lose its focus, or to placate a risk-averse client: instead challenge your copywriter to make the work as good as it can be.

Ask, how can we make this stronger? More potent, more exciting, more dramatic? How can we create something truly extraordinary and award-winning?

3. Be brave.

Take a deep breath: surprised by what you've read? Palms a bit sweaty?

Good. Not every bit of copy you get should make you nervous, but some of it should.

Being creative means doing something new. Doing something different. And different can be scary. Great copy should evoke a visceral response, not a shrug of the shoulders. And don't over-analyse: the audience won't spend 20 minutes studying the headline, neither should you. Remember your first impression, your gut reaction to it.

4. Think bigger than the brief.

If a piece of copy is off brief, is it *automatically* wrong? The copy might be better than the brief. If you just look at whether something is on brief, ticks every box or not, then you may be missing the bigger picture. First of all, is it a great piece of work?

If it's off brief because the copywriter has forgotten something important or been lazy, that's one thing. But if it's just better than the brief, embrace it.

5. Think about the audience.

Giving feedback shouldn't be about what you like, it should be about what you think will persuade the audience – so put yourself in their shoes.

Don't tell a copywriter you 'don't like it'. Good creative work is designed for a specific target audience – one you're unlikely to be. And the work wasn't even designed for the audience to 'like' – it was designed for them to respond to.

6. Don't solve the problem.

Don't say, "This sentence needs to change from this to this".

Get the copywriter to solve the problem. If someone else amends the copy, it'll end up with multiple voices and it won't flow very well. Besides, the copywriter is supposed to be the expert, so they should be able to come up with the best solution. That's what they're being paid for, after all.

In the introduction to this book, I pointed out that most people wouldn't dream of telling their plumber how to fit the new boiler.

Yet despite a similar lack of experience and expertise in copywriting, they'll happily comment on your work with all the vigour of Gordon Ramsay critiquing an oven chip.

Like any occupation that has an artistic aspect in a commercial world, you need thick skin to be a copywriter.

You need to know that just because someone's criticising your work, it doesn't necessarily mean your work's bad. It may just be that the person criticising it doesn't know what the hell they're talking about.

Either way, try not to take it personally. It may feel like a criticism of you or your ability or judgement, but it isn't. It's just a person disagreeing with your choice of words.

Death by a thousand cuts

Here's an experience you might be familiar with: round after round of amends. And while no one amend is significant, they add up. One problem is the way some organisations are set up to review work. About eight different people in different departments, at different levels, have to approve the work.

So eight copies of your copy go out. And two things happen.

First, people are being asked to perform a task: to review some copy. And how can they demonstrate that they've done that task and done it thoroughly? By making an amend or two. To leave it untouched looks like you haven't been through it properly. So unnecessary amends get made.

Second, you get the copy back with eight different people's thoughts annotated on it. Making it virtually impossible to retain a single tone of voice.

(Incidentally, if *you're* reviewing someone's copy, remember this: sometimes the bravest, best thing you can do is not change anything. To look at a piece of copy and say 'It may not be how I would have personally done it... but I recognise that it's on brief, well written and a strong piece of work. I'm going to leave it unscathed.')

So what can you do when the amends come in?

1: Are they right?

It's easy to be 'precious' as a copywriter. To be overly-protective of what you've written. But the truth is:

i) Your copy is one solution to the challenge. There are a million other ways to approach it, and many are likely to be at least as good as the one you've chosen.

ii) Being forced to go back and look at your copy with fresh eyes will, though it's hard to admit, almost always make it better.

iii) The person making the amend may be right. What they're suggesting may be better – because you're not going to be 100% right, 100% of the time.

So have an open mind and consider the pros and cons as objectively as you can. Compare their comments with the proposition, the objectives, the brand. Explore the possibility that the amend – or at least the intention behind it – may be valid.

2: Are they wrong?

For the amends you don't agree with, you need to know the strength of the client's feeling on them. Some 'amends' are actually just gentle musings, and if challenged, the client will say, "Oh it was only a suggestion, I don't mind if you want to leave it."

Others they will be adamant about. Some may be things that they as a business can't say – because it just goes against company policy or because it's something they have a bee in their bonnet about.

So don't be too quick to suggest, "That's a bad amend and you're a bloody idiot." They're not likely to agree (believe me, I've tried). It'll probably just make them more entrenched and insist you make the amend as it is.

i. Ask for the problem, not the solution

Clients will often mark up amends, literally what needs to change. If that's because of factual inaccuracies or legal requirements, then fine.

But if they're re-writing sentences (or paragraphs) then that's not fine. What they've written is unlikely to fit with everything around it.

So instead, get them to express their concerns and find out what they feel isn't right and what they want to achieve that currently the copy isn't doing. Echo it back to them, to ensure you both have the same understanding, then you can make the amend as sympathetically with the existing copy as possible.

ii. Have a solution in mind, not just an argument

Just as they should tell you the problem not the solution, you should have an idea for what you could do instead or differently from what they're suggesting. Just saying "No, that won't work" doesn't really help. Discussing what would work may.

iii. Have expertise and experience, not an opinion

When it comes to copy, your opinion should carry weight. *Should.* But a debate can quickly become a group of people giving their views, with everyone's views considered equal.

Instead, back up your 'opinions' with some facts based on your experience.

For example: "Well, we can do that, but it will make the headline four words longer – and I think the Viacom Outdoor research showed that any poster headline over 8 words long is 25% less likely to be read. What if I can find another way to get across your point without lengthening the headline?"

iv. Lose the battle, win the war

Choose your battles. Inevitably, some amends that you don't agree with will get made. See which ones you can live with. A bit of give and take will help your case with the ones you really don't agree with, rather than just saying *no* to all of them.

3. How to minimise amends

i. Get to know your client

If your clients know you they'll often behave a lot more humanly. Instead of saying, "Change this to that", they'll say, "What do you think about this?"

ii. Talk to the right person

You often get amends that come from a junior client, passed on from a senior client.

And that junior client finds it hard to listen to your protestations, because that would basically require them to go back to their boss and say, "I'm not going to make your amend like you asked." Which no junior client wants to do.

So, get the most senior relationship you can. The more senior the client, the more they'll be able to listen to your thoughts and alternative suggestions.

iii. Get them enthusiastic

Whoever you're dealing with, get them as enthusiastic about the work as you can. They'll be your work's advocate when you're not around – so try and instil a passion for what you've done.

iv. Get them to buy it before they've bought it

Severe amends are sometimes a consequence of misunderstandings. What you've given the client is either not what they were expecting, or they just didn't know what to expect.

Get agreement from the client on what you're going to do, and have early discussions with them on what you're thinking. 'Tissue meetings', they're sometimes called.

Then when you're selling the work, build it up before you reveal it. Recap the brief and the proposition and the story behind how you approached it. And describe it all in a way which means that the work, when you finally unveil it, is clearly the best solution to everything you've said. So you've got them persuaded before they've even read it.

And remember, good work does not 'sell itself'. Just as a great product needs your great copy to sell it, your great copy needs a great advocate to sell it.

Make sure more time is spent on selling the work properly and you'll spend less time on amending it into an ugly Frankenstein's monster that no-one's happy with.

At the end of the day

At the end of the day, it gets dark. Ho ho.

No, I have three final thoughts about amends and criticism:

1. It's easy to get caught up in the heat of the moment and fight against an amend which, when all's said and done, may be pretty minor. Don't harm the relationship over whether it should be a colon or semi-colon.

2. However, it's easy to go the other way and say yes to everything. Not only is this likely to ruin your copy, it also conveys a lack of pride and confidence in your work. If you make every change without a murmur, your client will start wondering if you know what you're doing.

3. It's not your copy. It's theirs. They paid you for it. (That's why I had to ask each client for permission to show 'my' work in the *Examples* section – because the clients own it, even though I wrote it.)

This is not art. This is business – and the client is paying for your words. Stand up for what you've done, of course. But if, after discussion and collaboration, they still want it the way they want it, give it to them.

You may say, "Why have a dog and bark yourself?" but if they insist on barking, you may have to go with it. If you refuse point-blank every time, you'll probably just lose the client. And believe me, that's not a good feeling.

5.4

Getting better

Hey, you've read this book. Which means you're already probably better than you were.

And better prepared than those copywriters yet to read it.

You want to get even better? Good for you.

When interviewing a copywriting candidate, David Ogilvy used to ask them what relevant books they'd read.

He was appalled when many of them said they hadn't read any, claiming they preferred to rely on their own talent instead.

He pointed out that you'd hardly put your life in the hands of a surgeon who'd never studied anatomy, who was just going to rely on their own instincts.

As we reach the end of our time together, I'll finish with the six things I think are important for any copywriter who wants to get better:

1. Be like Henry Ford

Lots of people work hard(ish) to get 'pretty decent' at something and then take their foot off the gas. But have you ever noticed that the best people in their field continue to work hard and strive hard even *after* they've got to the top?

Sometimes, if I've got a meeting somewhere distant, I have to get up early. And of course, there are fewer cars on the road at that time. But do you know what? The ones that you do see tend to be more expensive. You see a higher ratio of executive saloons at 6:30am than you do at 8:30am.

Why is that? Perhaps the best people *continue* to be the first in and last out of the office.

Someone once suggested to Henry Ford that he'd been lucky.

"Yes, I have been lucky," he replied. "And I find the harder I work, the luckier I get."

Or how about this cheesy phrase: 'The difference between *try* and *triumph* is a little *umph*.'

2. Be a jack of all trades...

In this book there's recommended reading covering typography, grammar, layout, psychology and more.

Learn about everything that might come into contact with your copywriting without necessarily being *about* copywriting.

My first job out of uni was working in a telemarketing team. It taught me a lot about how to grab someone's attention and how to best phrase an offer, to get the most people saying yes.

My second job was in the print buying team of a big marketing department. I learned loads about printing processes, paper stocks, production techniques, formats and so on. It's been useful ever since.

It's a hoary old cliché, but copywriters do tend to have a wide range of interests. Being a copywriter means you end up learning bits and bobs about all sorts of subjects. It helps make you a more rounded writer, with a better understanding of people and more interesting things to say.

3. ...and a master of some

Yes, be a jack of all trades – but have one or two things that you really specialise in. Be the best all-rounder you can be *and* the best specialist you can be. Specialise in long copy. Or headlines. Or digital copy. Or automotive copy. Or FMCG copy. Or witty copy. Or poetic copy.

You'll find it more rewarding to have an area you can really own, copy you'll win awards for.

4. Work with the best

You'll get better when you work with people who are better than you. People you can learn from. People you can compete against. People who will challenge you. And people who will support you too.

If you're working as a team in an agency and your art director is lazy or useless or both, find a way to motivate them and improve them. Or find someone else to work with.

No copywriter is an island and you need the best people around you to bring out the best in your copy. If you can't get that where you currently work, maybe you should work somewhere else.

5. Be demanding

Of yourself: of course. Kind of covered that in the first 'work hard' point. But be demanding of the people you work with too. Let them know that it matters to you, how good a job you do as a team. That passion can be infectious.

Unless you're part of a team whose members challenge one another and speak up when someone's not doing their bit, you're unlikely to achieve your potential. You'll all smile at one another, take it in turns to make the tea, nod approvingly at each other's decent-but-unspectacular contribution… and end up with some good work.

But not great work.

6. Enjoy it

Yes, predictable I know. But enjoying it *is* important. As someone wise once said, "When you enjoy what you do, nothing is work."

The preceding five points will come to you a lot more easily if you're enjoying what you do. Yes, of course there'll be days when someone or something is driving you mad. But overall, being a copywriter is a pretty fabulous job.

Sometimes you get people telling you how much they like what you've done (and there are many jobs where people never get told anything like that).

Sometimes you get to go to awards shows.

You get paid pretty well, you get to be creative – and you create something tangible that you can show other people as a result of your efforts.

And you'll always be in demand – because there just aren't that many good copywriters around.

Yep, being a copywriter is a pretty good gig. So be happy you've got that opportunity, make the most of it and enjoy it. And tell everyone you know to buy this book, so they can see just how much effort and skill goes into what you do.

Okay. Go be brilliant. Used to be, there were lots of great copywriters around. Now, not so much. Go be the next one.

I look forward to hearing about you.

BEYOND
THE WRITTEN WORD

Authors who speak to you face to face.

Discover LID Speakers, a service that enables businesses to have direct and interactive contact with the best ideas brought to their own sector by the most outstanding creators of business thinking.

- A network specialising in business speakers, making it easy to find the most suitable candidates.

- A website with full details and videos, so you know exactly who you're hiring.

- A forum packed with ideas and suggestions about the most interesting and cutting-edge issues.

- A place where you can make direct contact with the best in international speakers.

- The only speakers' bureau backed up by the expertise of an established business book publisher.